D0053419

THE
THANK YOU
ECONOMY

also by gary vaynerchuk

Gary Vaynerchuk's 101 Wines:
Guaranteed to Inspire, Delight,
and Bring Thunder to Your World

Crush It!:
Why NOW Is the Time to
Cash In on Your Passion

THE
THANK YOU
ECONOMY

gary vaynerchuk

HARPER
BUSINESS

An Imprint of HarperCollins*Publishers*
www.harpercollins.com

HarperCollins books may be purchased for educational, business, or sales promotional use. For information, please write: Special Markets Department, HarperCollins Publishers, 10 East 53rd Street, New York, NY 10022.

Designed by William Ruoto

Library of Congress Cataloging-in-Publication Data
Vaynerchuk, Gary.
    The thank you economy / Gary Vaynerchuk. 1st ed.
        p.   cm.
Includes bibliographical references.
ISBN: 978-0-06-191418-8 (hbk.)
ISBN: 978-0-06-209000-3 (B & N edition)
ISBN: 978-0-06-191424-9 (pbk.)
1. Customer relations.   2. Social media.
3. Branding (Marketing)   4. Internet
marketing.   5. Management.   I. Title.
HF5415.5.V396 2011
658.8'12—dc22   2010052581

11 12 13 14 15   OV/RRD   10 9 8 7 6

To my family and friends, but especially to Lizzie and Misha, the two girls who make me want to breathe.

"This 'telephone' has too many shortcomings to be seriously considered as a means of communication."

—Western Union internal memo, 1876

"The wireless music box has no imaginable commercial value. Who would pay for a message sent to nobody in particular?"

—an investor in response to David Sarnoff's push for radio, 1920

"While theoretically and technically television may be feasible, commercially and financially it is an impossibility."

—Lee De Forest, radio pioneer, 1926

"Visionaries see a future of telecommuting workers, interactive libraries and multimedia classrooms. They speak of electronic town meetings and virtual communities. Commerce and business will shift from offices and malls to networks and modems. And the freedom of digital networks will make government more democratic. Baloney."

—Cliff Stoll, author, astronomer, professor, 1995

"If I had a nickel for every time an investor told me this wouldn't work . . ."

—Jeff Bezos, founder of Amazon

CONTENTS

ACKNOWLEDGMENTS

Many people helped make this book what it is, but I want to especially thank Debbie Stier, Stephanie Land, and Marcus Krzastek. These three are as much the backbone of this book as I am.

I also want to thank everyone at HarperBusiness, VaynerMedia, the amazing people at the Brooks Group, and all my friends who took the time to read for me.

Many thanks to all of my family and friends for their support, especially my mom, Tamara, and dad, Sasha, who are always in my corner. Without my dad's courage, I would not be in this wonderful country, or where I am today. Also thanks to my amazing sister, Elizabeth, whom I truly admire; my wonderful brother, AJ, who is my best friend forever; my wife and daughter, who make me never want to leave in the morning, and always want to rush home; and my grandmother Esther—I love you.

I'm also grateful to my extended family—my brothers-in-law, Alex and Justin, who are just the best; my wonderful sister-in-law, Sandy, whom we just welcomed into the family; and my amazing in-laws, Anne and Peter, who are truly golden people. Peter, I hope all your friends and business acquaintances read this book.

Thanks to Bobby Shifirn and Brandon Warnke, who are my friends for life. To all the Vayniacs and supporters of what I do, you mean the world to me!

Can I thank Stephanie Land one more time? Best ghost writer in the world. I adore her.

've been living the Thank You Economy since a day sometime around 1995, when a customer came into my dad's liquor store and said, "I just bought a bottle of Lindemans Chardonnay for $5.99, but I got your $4.99 coupon in the mail. Can you honor it? I've got the receipt." The store manager working the floor at the time replied, "No." I looked up from where I was on my knees dusting the shelves and saw the guy's eyes widen as he said, "Are you serious?" The manager said, "No, no. You have to buy more to get it at $4.99." As the man left, I went over to the manager and said, "That guy will never come back." I was wrong about that; he did come back. He came back a couple of months later—to tell us he would never shop with us again.

Now, I wasn't any nicer than this manager, nor have I ever been a softie when it comes to business. However, though I was young and still had a lot to learn, I knew deep in my gut that he had made the wrong call. The manager believed he was protecting the store from a customer trying to take advantage of it; all

I could see was that we had missed an opportunity to make a customer happy.

Make no mistake: I've always seen business as a way to build a legacy, and a way to make people happy, but I've also been in the game to make money, not just to spread sunshine and rainbows. I'm the kid who ripped people's flowers out of their yards and sold them back to their owners. My incentive to make that customer happy wasn't purely altruistic; it was that happy customers are worth a lot more than any other kind. It was grounded in my belief at the time that a business is only as strong as its closest customer relationships, and that what those customers said about our business beyond our four walls would shape our future.

I didn't write *The Thank You Economy* to encourage businesses and brands to be nicer to their customers. I wrote it because what I believed was true back then is turning out to be even truer today. I'm intuitive that way. It's why I knew I should sell all my baseball cards and go into toy collectibles; why I launched WineLibrary.com in 1997 when nobody thought local liquor stores belonged online; why I decided to go all in on Australian and Spanish wines in 1999 when everyone else was still obsessed with France, California, and Italy. It's how I knew to use Twitter from the get-go, and that video blogging was going to be a big deal. And it's why I know I'm right now.

I want people who love running businesses and building businesses as much as I do—whether they're entrepreneurs, run a small business, or work for a Fortune 100 company—to understand what early adopters like me can already see—that we have entered a new era in which developing strong consumer relationships is pivotal to a brand or company's success. We have been pushing our message for too many decades. It's no longer enough that a strong marketing initiative simply funnels a brand's one-way message down the consumer's throat. To have an impact, it will have to inspire an emotionally charged interaction.

Just as open, honest communication is the key to good interpersonal relationships, so is it intrinsic to a brand or business's relationships with its customers. People embraced social media because communicating makes people happy; it's what we do. It's why we carved pictures into rocks. It's why we used smoke signals. It's why ink won. And if someone ever develops a tool that allows us to communicate telepathically, we'll be all over that, too. How businesses will adapt to that kind of innovation, I have no idea. But they will, I'm sure. At least, the ones I am associated with will.

In the meantime, companies of all stripes and sizes have to start working harder to connect with their customers and make them happy, not because change is coming, but because it's here. Imagine how many more people would have heard that we'd lost an unhappy customer's business if the man who couldn't get his coupon redeemed at Wine Library all those years ago had had a cell phone loaded with a Twitter and Facebook app. What's more, the changes we've already seen are just the first little bubbles breaking on the water's surface. The consumer Web is just a baby—many people reading this right now can probably clearly remember the world pre-Internet. The cultural changes social media have ushered in are already having a big impact on marketing strategies, but eventually, companies that want to compete are going to have to change their approach to everything, from their hiring practices to their customer service to their budgets. Not all at once, mind you. But it will have to happen, because there is no slowing down the torpedo-like speed with which technology is propelling us into the Thank You Economy. I, for one, think that's a good thing. By the time you're done with this book, I hope you'll agree.

PART I

Welcome to the Thank You Economy

CHAPTER ONE

How Everything Has Changed, Except Human Nature

Think back on the last time someone did something nice for you. I don't mean just holding the door open; I mean watching your dogs while you were away for the weekend or driving forty minutes to pick you up at the airport. How did you feel afterward? Grateful, maybe even damn lucky to know someone who would go out of his way like that for you. If given the chance, you'd be sure to reciprocate. You might not even wait to be given a chance—you might just do something to make him happy, and show your gratitude, because you could. Most of us recognize that to have someone like that in our life is a gift, one that shouldn't be taken for granted.

In fact, no relationships should be taken for granted. They are what life is all about, the whole point. How we cultivate our relationships is often the greatest determinant of the type of life we get to live. Business is no different. Real business isn't done in board meetings; it's done over a half-eaten plate of buffalo wings at the sports bar, or during the intermission of a Broadway show. It's done through an enthusiastic greeting, with an unexpected recommendation, or by offering up your cab when it's raining. It happens in the small, personal interactions that allow us to prove to each other who we are and what we believe in, honest moments that promote good feelings and build trust and loyalty. Now imagine you could take those interactions and scale them to the hundreds, thousands, or even millions of people who make up your customer base, or better yet, your potential customer base. A lot of people would insist that achieving that kind of scale is impossible, and up until about five years ago, they would have been right. Now, though, scaling those interactions is not only possible—provided you use the right tools the right way—it's necessary. In fact, those companies and brands that refuse to try could jeopardize the potential of their business, and in the long term, even their very existence.

Why? Because when it comes down to it, the only thing that will never change is human nature. When given the choice, people will always spend their time around people they like. When it's expedient and practical, they'd also rather do business with and buy stuff from people they like. And now, they can. Social media has made it possible for consumers to interact with businesses in a way that is often similar to how they interact with their friends and family. Early tech adopters jumped on the chance to regularly talk to businesses, and as time goes by, more and more people are getting excited by the idea and following their lead. You may not have seen the effects of this movement yet, but I have. I see them every day. Trusting relationships and connections formed via social media are quickly becoming two subtle but rapidly growing forces of our economy. It is imperative that brands and businesses learn how to properly and authentically use social media to develop one-to-one relationships with their customer base—no matter how big—so that they make an impact in their market, now and in the future.

Social Media Is More than Media

For the record, I dislike the term "social media." It is a misnomer that has caused a boatload of confusion. It has led managers, marketers, CEOs, and CMOs to think they can use social networking sites to spread their message the same way they use traditional media platforms like print, radio, television, or outdoor, and expect similar results and returns. But what we call social media is not media, nor is it even a platform. It is a massive cultural shift that has profoundly affected the way society uses the greatest platform ever invented, the Internet. Unfortunately, when the business world is thinking about marketing via social networking sites like YouTube, Facebook, Twitter, Foursquare, and DailyBooth, it's thinking about using social media, so that's the term I'll use, too.

Great News Is in the Eye of the Beholder

Finally, a way to really connect with our customers, an opportunity to hear what they want, what they think, how things went, how our product worked, or how it didn't! At last, a chance to create personal and creative campaigns that do more than shove our message down our customers' collective throats! Don Draper would have dropped his whiskey glass in joyful delirium if you had told him that his agency didn't have to run focus groups anymore to find out what people wanted. Think of all the money that brand managers could have saved over the decades on test marketing and other classic research techniques which, in all these years, haven't done much to improve a new product's risk of failure, estimated at 60 to 90 percent; they'd be looking cross-eyed at today's social media marketing skeptics for not recognizing great news when they hear it. But, shockingly, a lot of people don't want to hear it. If it's true that one-to-one is quickly becoming one of the most important ways to reach customers, then it means a massive number of businesses are eventually going to have to undergo a total cultural transformation to compete. That's a thought most corporate execs are going to meet with about as much enthusiasm as Dwyane Wade would if he were suddenly faced with undeniable proof that basketball was dead and ice hockey was the only game left.* Yet let's remember it wasn't so long ago that the few people who owned home computers used them almost exclusively for word processing and video games. In 1984, you'd get stuffed in your locker for gloating over your new Apple Macintosh; in 2007 you could score a hot date by showing off your new iPhone. Culture changes, and business has to change with it or die.

---

* In the early drafts of this manuscript I referred to LeBron James here, but as you sports fans know . . . things change.

Why I Speak in Absolutes

Because if I give you an inch, you'll run a mile with it. When I said in 1998, "You're dead if you don't put your business on the Internet and get in on ecommerce," was that true? No. But boy, can you imagine trying to be in business in 2010 with zero Web presence? I'd rather shock you into paying attention, and admit later that business rarely requires an all-or-nothing approach, than take the chance that you won't take the situation seriously enough.

Unfortunately, a lot of business leaders and marketing professionals can't see that change is here. (Not coming. Not around the corner. *Here.*) They look at the business being done on Twitter, Facebook, myYearbook, and Foursquare, and say with contempt, "Prove it."

My pleasure. In this book, you'll read about an array of big and small companies, in a variety of industries, that were proud to share how they successfully improved their bottom line by leveraging and scaling the relationships made possible by social media. When looked at as a whole, these examples offer undeniable evidence that there is financial gain for any size company that is willing to open the lines of communication with its customers and market to them in a personal, caring way that makes them feel valued. There's no reason why any company couldn't make these efforts and achieve similar results. Social media makes the Internet an open, level playing field where any limits to how far you want to spread your message and your brand are self-imposed.

The secret to these companies' success is that at some level, they figured out how to put into practice a number of the ideas I want to explain in this book:

- The building blocks necessary to create a powerful, legacy-building company culture
- How to re-create the perfect date when developing your traditional and social media strategies
- Using good intent to set everything in motion
- Delivering shock and awe to your customers without investing a lot of money, just a whole lot of heart

In addition, they weren't held back by fear or the arguments many leaders use to dismiss the effectiveness of social media. In this book, I'll tackle the most common of those arguments and explain why they don't hold water.

Consumer expectations are changing dramatically, and social media has altered everything about how companies must— MUST—relate to their customers. From now on, the relationship between a business and a customer is going to look very different from the way it has looked in the recent past.

The Heart and Soul of the Matter

How do people decide they like each other? They talk. They exchange ideas. They listen to each other. And eventually, a relationship forms. The process is no different for building relationships with customers. If your organization's intentions transcend the mere act of selling a product or service, and it is brave enough to expose its heart and soul, people will respond. They will connect. They will like you. They will talk. They will buy.

A survey of parents preparing for the fall 2010 back-to-school shopping season found that 30 percent of them expected that social networking would affect their purchases; another survey, conducted in early December 2009, revealed that 28 percent said their buying decisions had been affected by social networking, with 6 percent admitting to being influenced by a friend's Facebook status about a product and 3 percent being influenced by a friend's tweet. By the time you're reading this book, the percentages will be dramatically higher. More and more, people are making business and consumer decisions based on what they see talked about on social media platforms. The thing is, people don't talk about things they don't care about. So it's up to you to make them care, which means you have to care first.

When I first started tweeting, I had no brand recognition; no one knew who I was. To build my brand, I started creating conversations around what I cared passionately about: wine. I used Search.Twitter (called Summize.com back then) to find mentions of Chardonnay. I saw that people had questions, and I answered them. I didn't post a link to WineLibrary.com and point out that I sold Chardonnay. If people mentioned that they were drinking Merlot, I gave them my Merlot recommendation, but I didn't mention that they could buy Merlot on my website. I didn't try to close too early, like a nineteen-year-old guy; I made sure to invest in the relationship first. Eventually, people started to see my comments and think, "Oh, hey, it's that Vaynerchuk guy; he knows Chardonnay. Oh cool, he does a wine show—let's take a look. Hey, he's funny. I like him; I trust him. And check it out: he sells wine, too. Free shipping? Let's try a bottle of that. . . ." That's what caring first, not selling first, looks like, and that's how I built my brand.

That's what I mean about revealing your company's heart and soul. There's only so low you can go on price. There's only so excellent you can make your product or service. There's only so far you can stretch your marketing budget. Your heart, though— that's boundless. Maybe it doesn't sound realistic to expect anyone to be that emotional in business, but hey, how many people thought they would be tending to a virtual farm three years ago? Meanwhile, at its peak Farmville saw 85 million players.

Now, I realize that your reality isn't boundless; scaling one-to-one relationships and hiring employees to help you costs money and time. But in this book, I'll show you that when you spend money on social media, you're not actually investing in a platform—you're investing in a culture, and in consumers who can ultimately become your ambassadors. We'll examine the return on investment and talk about how to make every dollar count. Ideally, though, your goal should be "No Interaction Left Behind," because what pays off most is your willingness to show people that you care—about them, about their experience with you, about their business.

It's not as hokey as it sounds. In fact, it is exactly how the business world used to run. I believe that we are living through the early days of a dramatic cultural shift that is bringing us back full circle, and that the world we live and work in now operates in a way that is surprisingly similar to the one our great-grandparents knew. Social media has transformed our world into one great big small town, dominated, as all vibrant towns used to be, by the strength of relationships, the currency of caring, and the power of word of mouth. In order to succeed now and in the future, it's going to be imperative that we remember what worked in the past.

When Caring Meant Business

If you're lucky enough to spend any time around any eighty- or ninety-year-olds who still have their wits about them and their memory intact, you'll inevitably hear them remark how much the world has changed since they were young. Most elderly people can easily identify many ways in which the world has changed for the better, but they often express more than a hint of regret for a time when things moved more slowly, when people knew their neighbors, and when strangers and friends alike were expected to treat each other with courtesy and respect (even if they didn't feel like it). They'll also reminisce about how retailers and local businesses made it a point to know your name and make you feel like family when you walked in. As well they should have. Whether you lived in a small town or one of the small-town communities re-created in city neighborhoods, it was entirely possible the business owners/managers had known you your whole life.

Back then, there was no need to encourage people to buy local. Local was, for the most part, all there was. If your mother bought her meat at Butcher Bob's, it was pretty likely that you shopped at Butcher Bob's, too. Butcher Bob knew your family, knew your tastes, and knew that during the cold months he should reserve a hambone for you to flavor your weekly batch of split-pea soup. How Butcher Bob treated you when you walked into his store was as crucial as the quality of his ground beef. It wasn't that you only had to walk three blocks over to see what rival Butcher Bill had to offer in his case. It was that if you weren't happy with the service you received—if, for example, Butcher Bob refused to reimburse you for the freshly ground chuck that you brought home only to discover it wasn't so fresh—you'd vent your outrage to the PTA, or a trade union meeting, or the country club. That was Butcher Bob's worst nightmare, if the PTA, trade unions, or country club members represented a big chunk of his customer base. To lose one disgruntled customer could often mean losing ten of his or her friends and relatives. In the smaller, tight-knit communities of yesteryear, ten people represented a lot of revenue. Businesses lived and died by what was said via word of mouth, and by the influence people had with one another. That meant every person who walked through the door had to feel as though he or she mattered. Unless he was the only game in town, the butcher, the baker, the candlestick maker—heck, everyone who had to deal with customers—had to be as friendly, accommodating, and, when necessary, apologetic as the other guy, if not more so.

This was an era when businesses could stay in family hands for several generations. Often, the business wasn't just a way to make money; it was something the owners and managers closely identified with and in which they took pride. When the business was relatively new, the people who ran it often cared as though their life depended upon it because, well, it did. The business was their ticket to the American dream. This is what was going to launch their children's future. They were in it for the long haul; it would be their legacy. And in the end, when they retired, they were probably still going to live among all the people with whom they had done business for many years. Their customers weren't just walking wallets; they were friends and neighbors, so business owners cared about their customers. A lot.

Word of Mouth Loses Its Voice

That world our grandparents and great-grandparents knew, the one where relationships and word of mouth could have a direct impact on an individual's personal and professional reputation, and on the success or failure of one's business, began to disintegrate around the time when ordinary people like Butcher Bob bought their first car, in the years between the mid-to-late 1920s and the post–World War II boom. Around the middle of the last century, a whole lot of social and economic forces converged, and people took advantage of their affordable cars and the new highways built for them to head out to suburbia. As time went on, Americans started fleeing even farther, to exurbia. The countryside was paved with parking lots and lined with strip malls to serve the burgeoning commuter society. For many, the sign that you'd arrived was that you had managed to put as much distance as possible between yourself and everybody else, preferably with a gate.

These decades that brought greater distance between friends, family, and neighbors coincided with the rapid rise of big business. Butcher Bob retired just in time to avoid being crushed by the newly built Safeway supermarket chain, which would eventually include over two thousand stores across the country. If the company that treated Great-Grandma like royalty even when she was only buying a two-dollar hat had grown and prospered, in all probability a corporation gobbled it up. Eventually its reason for being became less about delighting the ladies with the newest fashions, or building a legacy, and more about satisfying quarterly returns and improving stock options. The prioritization of profit over principle quickly took over American corporate culture and is what shaped the perspective of all ranks of many of today's business leaders. Most have never known anything else. They're just playing the game as they were taught.

If You Don't Care, No One Will

What happened next is almost forgivable. Almost. After all, consumers seemed to have rejected old-world values and abandoned small-town or community-oriented businesses. Plus, in the wake of a variety of social and cultural upheavals, manners took a nosedive. It was definitely time to ditch some of the fussy formalities society had long been saddled with, but manners— real manners—indicate that we care about other people's feelings, and about their experience when they're around us. It was almost as if big business looked around, took note of the increasingly relaxed social norms, and thought, "Well, shoot, if they don't care, neither do we." If people were going to expect very little, little is what they were going to get.

Companies started unloading anything that didn't immediately and directly track to pumping up their bottom line. It wasn't just about replacing the hats with cheaper, more modern fashions. Nor did it mean simply phasing out little extras that made a customer feel like royalty. It meant power bombing anything that showed the company cared about the customer experience at all. Supermarkets stopped hiring teenagers to load bags and carry them to the car. Gas station attendants disappeared except in New Jersey and Oregon. And if you wanted to speak to a company about their product or service, you could press 1 to spell your name, press 2 to place an order, press 3 for more options, or press the star key to return to the main menu. As the 1980s rolled into the 1990s and companies relied increasingly on automated call centers, we were ushered into a customer service dark ages.

People griped and moaned, but there was nothing they could do. Some even swallowed the company lie that eliminating the unnecessary, time-consuming, expensive perks that customers used to take for granted—such as the privilege of speaking to a live human being—made it possible to keep prices down. We loved talking to you, but our loss is your gain. Enjoy the savings!

The Internet only made everything worse. For all its globalizing properties, it allowed us to take our isolationism even further. Now we didn't even have to go to the mall to do our shopping or the megaplex to see a movie. No matter where we lived, in fact, with the click of a mouse we could bring the world—or rather, the world as we wanted to see it, with a selection of entertainment, politics, and media cherry-picked to meet our individual tastes—straight to us without ever having to speak to another live human being. We could order our groceries online. We never had to leave the house. We could conceivably become a community of one.

For business, our Internet love affair was a gift from the gods. Online startups exploded and the target markets for existing companies dramatically expanded. Businesses could now point proudly to their websites and assure their customers that the lines of communication would never close. In theory, the website made them available 24/7. In reality, with a few exceptions, these corporate websites merely made it that much easier to truly pander to the idea of service without actually providing any. In fact, it made it possible for them to virtually avoid dealing with customers altogether. Now people could waste even more time clicking around on websites in a fruitless effort to find a phone number or the name of someone to speak with. When all that was available was an email address, they could send out a question, complaint, or comment into the ether and wait God knows how long until receiving a totally bland, formulaic, and useless reply. In the event they could dig up a phone number, they wasted millions, maybe even billions of hours per year on hold, or being transferred from one helpless or hapless rep to another. As companies outsourced their customer service, customers struggled to make themselves understood by script-reading foreigners. They seethed, but as usual, there was nothing they could do.

Corporations had nothing to fear. Their customer base was no longer in the local zip codes within a five- or even fifteen-mile radius—it was the entire country, and in some cases, the whole world. So what if one person got her panties in a bunch? Or a hundred? How many people, realistically, were going to take the time to find sites like Paypalsucks.com, read them, post on them, and tell their friends? How many friends could they possibly tell, anyway? It just wasn't worth the time, money, or effort to handle each customer, whether satisfied or disgruntled, with anything other than a token bit of goodwill. The ROI didn't justify doing things any other way.

Small-Town Living Moves Online

Then, around 2003, in the midst of this high-tech, digital, impersonal world, a new train started bulleting across the online landscape. It was nothing like the trains our great-grandparents might have ridden, but for all its shiny digital modernity, in essence it closed the vast distances created over a near-century of car culture, cheap land, and technology. Many of us still lived far apart from one another, but we were about to be connected in a totally small-town way.

The train was Web 2.0, now known as social media. It rode along the rails of the Web at breathtaking speed, every one of its cars a powerful platform designed with the express purpose of getting people to talk to one another again. The silent, anonymous, private Internet suddenly turned extremely chatty, personal, and revealing. Small-town living moved online as people eagerly sought out each other's latest news. Our morning social media browse to check in on what everyone has been up to became the equivalent of the old-timers' early morning stroll to the diner for pancakes and coffee. We check Facebook and comment on a friend's photo of her new shoes (which we know without asking are Kate Spades and were bought at Nordstrom's because she said so in her status update) the same way we once would have remarked, "You look lovely in that hat, Margie," as we passed by our neighbor. We click "like" upon seeing our friend's status update announcing his kid's college graduation the same way we'd have nodded approvingly upon seeing that little Timmy had finally gotten the hang of his Radio Flyer scooter. We tweet an article and accompany it with some curses for the city management clowns bungling up yet another public works project with the same energy we'd use to rattle our newspaper and vent our frustration to all the other folks lined up next to us at the diner counter reading their paper, sipping their coffee—plain, black—and chewing on a doughnut.

Social media allowed us to become more aware of the minutiae in each other's lives, of what was going on, of what people were thinking and doing, than ever before. In the 1940s, we'd have found out about the progress of our neighbor's new wallpapering project or model ship during run-ins at the bus stop or the Piggly Wiggly. In 1990 we might not have known about these projects at all. And in 2010, we can not only know about them, we can see pictures and video chronicling their progress and get information about the retailers and service providers involved. In the beginning, a lot of people saw the banality of the topics flying around and wondered who could possibly care that Jeff

in Boulder had found a half-eaten bag of Snickers in the pan-
try, or that Liz in Miami was heading out to the beach for a run
in her new Pumas. But people did care. Society jumped on the
chance to re-create the regular exchanges of personal news and
thoughts that used to be a staple of those smaller, relationship-
based communities.

A Full-Circle Power Shift

Still, most businesses, save for some ambitious entrepreneurs,
didn't see any upside to jumping on that train. Where could it
possibly go that could be of use to them? Many leaders failed
to see—some of them still fail to see—that the game they all
learned to play has finally started to change. (Those changes are
going to be insane in five years!) By allowing dialogues to occur and relationships to grow on a daily basis, for free, between
people living as far apart as Des Moines and Osaka who might
never actually meet in person, social media represents a gigantic
power shift back to the consumer. Consumers have more direct,
daily contact with other consumers than has ever been possible
in the history of the planet. More contact means more sharing of
information, gossiping, exchanging, engaging—in short, more
word of mouth. Now, Jeff's friend on the other side of the country, whom he hasn't seen in six years and who has fast-forwarded
through every television commercial since getting his first DVR
in 2003, might see Jeff's post about the half-eaten Snickers, remember how much he likes that candy bar, and pick one up that
afternoon while waiting in the supermarket checkout line. That's

a plausible scenario that Great-Grandma could never have fore-seen.

How the New Word of Mouth Is Different

Word of mouth is back. When society cut the close personal and business ties that existed in older, smaller communities, people became like ants scattered around on a picnic table—really busy, really strong, but too far apart from one another to get much accomplished as a unit. Now, the Internet has ma-tured so that the power of social media can allow all the ants to collectively gather under the table, and they're strong enough to haul it away if they so choose. Any businessperson who can't see the repercussions of that much potential word of mouth has his or her eyes closed. For example, even if Martha isn't that interested in agriculture or the subject of genetically modified food, the fact that her friend in Hamburg *is* might be enough to make her pay attention when spotting a post on a social net-working or microblogging site (Twitter, Posterous, Tumblr) about the activities of some company called Monsanto. Maybe she reads the attached link and starts to form an opinion, and then reposts or retweets so that her two hundred friends can see why she feels the way she does. She then enjoys the heated conversation that ensues with the twenty-five people who re-ply. Of those twenty-five people, eighteen repost and retweet the original article, with a personal message attached, to their respective friends. According to Facebook, as of 2010, the av-erage Facebook user has 130 friends, and the average Twitter account holder has 300 followers, which in total add up to a potential 7,740 people who suddenly have Monsanto's name flying in front of their eyes. That doesn't even factor in the 175 people who had access to Martha's original post but didn't say anything to Martha about it. Some saw it, some didn't. But of those who did, who knows how many silently reposted it to people who might then, in turn, have reposted it? Think about how many thousands of people that represents. And, many of them did it immediately from the smartphone that goes everywhere they go. There's no more lag between the time someone hears, reads, or sees something and the time that person can get back to a computer and shoot out an email to a dozen friends. News and information that had always traveled fast, whether being transmitted in older, tiny communities via front porch or window ledge or in larger ones by balcony, fire escape, phone, or email, is now traveling across the world in real time. A crucial difference between the spread of information and opinion then and now, though, is that the recipients of that information and opinion more often care about the individual sending it to them. Middlemen, pundits, and spokespersons no longer have a near-monopoly on the widespread distribution of a brand or a company's message.

We talk more passionately about things we care about than about things toward which we are ambivalent. We listen more closely to people we care about than to people we do not know. And now, we are talking and listening in unprecedented numbers, and our opinions and purchasing decisions are being affected and influenced even as we stand in the store aisle and weigh our options.

A few months ago I was at Best Buy, and I watched as a teenager used his Facebook status to request recommendations on a Nintendo Wii game. He got feedback in real time, and used it to decide what to buy. Recommendations and contextual social search are the future. Is it any wonder I'm not bullish on search engine optimization's (SEO) long-term potential?

Businesses that aren't able or willing to join the conversation will likely see their balance sheets suffer, and catch hell from Wall Street. That's the best-case scenario. Worst case, they aren't going to be in business much longer.

Power to the People

Finally, when faced with bad service or unfair policies or plain old indifference, there is something people can do. Now if customers have a complaint that they can't get resolved via traditional channels, they can post a frustrated status update or tweet that could get passed along forever. Suddenly, everyone who's ever had a problem with a company can compare notes, work him- or herself up into a righteous frenzy, and build enough animosity via word of mouth to create a real PR nightmare. AT&T knows something about how this happens. Giorgio Galante, who took AT&T to task on his blog called *So Long, and Thanks for All the Fish**,

---

*   In the time since I first started writing about this story, Galante appears to have taken down his blog.

wrote two emails to AT&T CEO Randall Stephenson. The first he wrote after the company's customer service reps were unable to authorize his request for an early iPhone upgrade; the second was to express his dissatisfaction with AT&T's data rates. In reply, Galante received a voice mail from someone on the AT&T Executive Response Team threatening legal action should he try to contact the CEO again. He finally received (and accepted) an apology from a senior VP, but by then the damage had been done—the story had spread all over the Internet, and even CNN tried to interview him (a request that he declined). How many of the people following Galante decided right then and there that the second Verizon gets on the iPhone, they're switching, or that maybe their Droid phone wasn't so bad after all? Too many for AT&T's taste, I'm sure.

This example perfectly reflects the magnitude by which word of mouth has exploded. Five years ago, it wouldn't have mattered that this guy was upset. He would have told four people. So what? Maybe, if he were a heavy hitter, he would have told some fellow board members, one of whom could have mentioned it to a journalist friend, who would have written a story about it and forced the company to take the complaint seriously. But this would have been a rarity. The odds were that maybe one out of every million times someone complained about a company, the newspaper would pick it up. If there was a particularly juicy angle to the story, the chances were ten million to one that *Nightline* would pick it up, as in the case of Mona Shaw, who became a literal heavy hitter when she stormed her local Comcast office and smashed a customer service representative's computer and workspace with a hammer. But now? You don't have to have a juicy angle. You just have to care enough to talk about your experience, and everyone you know is going to rally, just as your friends in the PTA, the trade union, or the country club would have rallied if you'd vented your outrage at Butcher Bob's cheating ways. The story potentially makes its way onto hundreds of influential blogs, and suddenly AT&T has got a massive headache.

Everything is in reverse. Before, it made some financial sense for big business to simply ignore people they considered whiners and complainers. Now, dissatisfied, disappointed consumers have the power to make companies feel the pinch. What a shame that that's what it's going to take to make some executives take social media seriously! It means they're using it only to react to the potential harm it can do to their business. There's so much unbelievable good it can do, though, especially when companies use it proactively. Social media is a great tool for putting out fires, but it's an even better tool for building brand equity and relationships with your customers. Once you stop thinking about it as a tool for shutting customers up, and rather as a tool for encouraging customers to speak up, and for you to speak to them, a whole world of branding and marketing opportunities will unfold.

The Thank You Economy

At its core, social media requires that business leaders start thinking like small-town shop owners. They're going to have to take the long view and stop using short-term benchmarks to gauge their progress. They're going to have to allow the personality, heart, and soul of the people who run all levels of the business to show. And they're going to have to do their damndest to shape the word of mouth that circulates about them by treating each customer as though he or she were the most important customer in the world. In short, they're going to have to relearn and employ the ethics and skills our great-grandparents' generation took for granted, and that many of them put into building their own businesses. We're living in what I like to call the Thank You Economy, because only the companies that can figure out how to mind their manners in a very old-fashioned way—and do it authentically—are going to have a prayer of competing.

Note that I said you have to do it authentically. I am wired like a CEO and care a great deal about the bottom line, but I care about my customers even more than that. That's always been my competitive advantage. I approach business the same way I approach every talk I present—I bring this attitude whether I have an audience of ten or ten thousand. Everybody counts, and gets the best I have to give. A lot of the time, we call people who do a consistently great job "a professional," or "a real pro." I try to be a pro at all times, and I demand that everyone I hire or work with try to be one, too. All my employees have to have as much of that caring in their DNA as I do. How else do you think I outsell Costco locally and Wine.com nationally? It started with hustle, sure. I always say that the real success of Wine Library wasn't due to the videos I posted, but to the hours I spent talking to people online afterward, making connections and building relationships. Yet I could have hustled my ass off and talked to a million people a day about wine, but if I or any of the people who represent Wine Library had come off as phonies or schmoozers, Wine Library would not be what it is today. You cannot underestimate the sharpness of people's BS radar—they can spot a soulless, bureaucratic tactic a million miles away. BS is a big reason why so many companies that have dipped a toe in social media waters have failed miserably there.

At Wine Library, we don't just pull out the charm when a big spender walks in, or when someone is unhappy, and we don't reply to inquiries with carefully worded legalese. We try not to calculate that one customer is worth more than another, and therefore worth more time and more effort, even as we recognize that a big customer can bring a lot to the table. How can you ever know who is potentially a big customer, anyway? Maybe you've got a customer who spends only a few hundred dollars with you a year. What you can't see is that the customer is spending a few thousand elsewhere, maybe with your competitor. You have no way of knowing that the customer's best friend is the biggest buyer in the category. Now, what if you were able to build a relationship, make a connection, tilt the person's emotions toward you, and capture 30, 60, or even 100 percent of what he or she spends? Your small customer would become a lot bigger. That's why you have to take every customer seriously. This is a basic business principle that has been talked and written about a great deal, and some companies take it seriously. But the playing field is so different now from, say, 1990, that companies can no longer treat it as a nice idea to which they should aspire. Valuing every single customer is mandatory in the Thank You Economy.

If there's a problem, we at Wine Library never tell ourselves that once we handle this issue, we'll never have to deal with the person again. We talk to every single person as though we're going to wind up sitting next to that person at his or her mother's house that night for dinner. We make it clear that we want to help in whatever way we can, and that everyone's business matters to us. And we mean it.

Sometimes, no matter how hard we try, we lose because someone else established the relationship first. For the most part, everyone has more than one place to find what it is you're selling. I've had people tell me that though they like what I do and live in my town, they buy from the other guy's liquor store because he's been good to them. I say, "I'm cheaper and I have a way better selection and I'll be good to you, too! Heck, I'll be better!" but I can't win, because a relationship has already been formed. I can compete on price, I can compete on convenience, and if they'd give me the chance I'd compete on caring, too. But they're not going to give me that chance unless the other guy slips up. And even then they'd probably give him a second chance, because forgiveness is the hallmark of a good relationship. If I kept pounding I might be able to win a percentage of my competitor's business, but the little guy in town will keep his consumer's market share with real caring and service.

Anyone working for a big company might be skeptical that a large business, or even a strictly online business, can form the same kind of friendly, loyal relationship with customers as a local retailer. I'm saying it's already been done because I lived it. I built my online company the same way I built the brick-and-mortar store. But it works only if everybody at the company gets on board, which is why unless you are building a new company from the ground up and can install caring as your business's cornerstone, you have to be willing to embark on a complete cultural overhaul so that, like a local mom-and-pop shop, every employee is comfortable engaging in customer service, and does it authentically. Your engagement has to be heartfelt, or it won't work.

A Gift to Customers and Companies

People want this level of engagement from the companies with which they do business. They always did, but they lost the power to demand it. Now they have it back, and they're indulging in that power. Even the best of what formerly passed for good customer service is no longer enough. You have to be no less than a customer concierge, doing everything you can to make every one of your customers feel acknowledged, appreciated, and heard. You have to make them feel special, just like when your great-grandmother walked into Butcher Bob's shop or bought her new hat, and you need to make people who aren't your customers wish they were. Social media gives businesses the tools to do that for the first time in a scalable way.

Platforms like Facebook and Twitter give back to businesses, too, in the form of real-time feedback. Companies can see for themselves when their lackluster advertising or weak marketing gets panned or ignored, and how their creative, engaging, authentic campaigns get praised and passed along. Even industries that have long resisted paying too close attention to metrics, such as newspaper editorial departments, are turning to online tracking tools to help them allocate resources and shape online content in blogs and podcasts. There doesn't need to be any guessing about how positively or negatively the public is responding to a brand when it's in the news or on TV—the public's reaction is often right there in black-and-white on Facebook, while the cameras are still rolling. In the Thank You Economy, social media allows us to get fresh, visceral, real-time feedback, not stale focus-group opinions. It blows my mind that so many companies resist social media. The fact that customers are open to speaking with them, not just to complain or to praise them but to initiate dialogue, offer opinions, and provide feedback, is fantastic! They should be on their knees with gratitude for the tremendous opportunity they now have to quickly (and cheaply) adapt and improve their strategies.

Exceed Expectations or Lose

Before, people were satisfied if you sent them an e-newsletter and the occasional 10-percent-off coupon in the mail. That was considered great customer engagement. Anything more was unheard of. Now, the standards have been raised by companies like Zappos, which will spend as much time on the phone with you as you need, and Fresh Direct, a New York online grocer that wraps your produce in bubble wrap and tucks an extra bunch of asparagus in with your order just to thank you for being such a great customer. Some retailers are known for charming their customers with thank you notes, like Hem in Austin, Texas—which also offers you wine or beer to drink while you shop—who sends them out a few days after you make your purchase. But how many online companies do it? Not many, which is why Wufoo, an online HTML form developer, gets so much blog coverage when its customers receive handwritten thank you notes, sometimes crafted out of construc-tion paper and decorated with stickers. What's extra special about the Wufoo notes is that they don't appear to be triggered by any particular purchase; they're sent out randomly to longtime cus-tomers, just to say "Thanks for doing business with us."

Now, it is true that the more you give, the more people want. It breaks my heart that I want to fly first class now. It's so much nicer, and now that I know what it's like, I want it all the time. I could travel that way regularly, but I don't, because I don't want to be that guy. The real question is, though, why can't everyone on the plane get first-class treatment, even the pas-sengers who are not paying for bigger seats? I think they even-tually will, because they're going to start demanding it. Not the perks—the warm nuts and Champagne, or even the bigger seats and leg room—but the respect? The kindness? Absolutely. All businesses, not just the airlines, need to start treating their consumers as though they're big spenders. My own father was worried about creating that kind of expectation at the liquor store, because where would it end? And what would happen if we stopped offering more? I had to work hard to convince him that if we didn't do it, someone else would. We built the first-class customer philosophy into the business, and people raved about us. They came back, they raved some more, their friends came to check us out, they raved about us, and through great customer service and word of mouth we built a large, loyal fan base. (Oh man, Wine Library would be so much bigger today, though, if the Thank You Economy had been in full force when we got started!) We'll talk later about what to do when people make unreasonable demands, but for the most part, the kind of service people are learning to expect isn't that shocking; companies just aren't used to having to give it.

Now, people expect you to give a damn about them. Not only that, they expect you to prove it. And the only way to prove it is to listen, engage, give them what they want when you can, and, when you can't, give them an honest answer why. They just want to be heard and taken seriously. That's all.

Engagement Is Not a Four-Letter Word

Tall order? Yep. A lot of work? Heck, yes. But companies no longer have a choice. I know that for many business leaders, investing in "engagement" is the same as eating a mouthful of cotton candy—it tastes sweet, but leaves you with a whole lot of nothing. However, I'm going to show that there is no more risk in allocating resources to perfecting your social media strategy than there is in screaming "Buy My Stuff!" on television, radio, in print, or on outdoor media. Then we'll focus on what needs to be in place for any company, whether big or small, B2B or B2C, cool or conventional, to use social media correctly to build one-to-one relationships. If you've already experimented with social media and it didn't work, there are only two possible reasons: your product or service isn't any good, or you're doing it wrong. We're going to assume your problem is the latter.

If there are any shortcomings in your brand or product, they might be starkly revealed once you start implementing so-

cial media correctly. Don't let this possibility stop you. Listen
to your customers' suggestions and complaints (as well as
their praise), and take the opportunity to fix the problem; then
use social media to show the world how you've changed and
improved.

I'll introduce some shining examples of what social media
done right looks like, and what it can help companies achieve in
an economy where an earnest, well-timed "thank you"—whether
it's in the form of a handshake, a comment, or a sample—is
worth as much to a business as a Platinum Amex. I'm going to
show you how incredibly far the effects of a sincerely expressed
"How may I help you?" or "What can I do for you?" or "You are
too kind." or "I'm so sorry. What can I do to make this right?"
or, perhaps most important, "I am so happy to hear from you!"
can take your business in a world where word of mouth travels
more quickly and holds more power than it ever has before. Suc-
ceeding in the Thank You Economy is not about simply being
nice and selling in an inoffensive way. Anyone can do that. It's
about taking every opportunity to show that you care about your
customers and how they experience your brand in a way that is
memorably and uniquely you.

What Caring Looks Like

Imagine you are the CEO of Super Duper Fans, Inc., sitting in
your local coffee shop, and you overhear one patron say to an-

other, "You know, you really get what you pay for. I'm trying to go green by not using my A/C so much, so I went out and bought a bunch of fans. I didn't want to spend a fortune, either, so I bought those Super Duper fans, the ones with that great ad on TV."

"Ooh, with the monkey? Yeah, I've seen them; they're hilarious!"

"I set them up and two are already broken. Figures, right? Piece of junk."

Any executive or manager or sales rep who cares about the company and believes in what it does wouldn't hesitate to approach the table, introduce him- or herself, defend the product, apologize for any inconvenience, and ask for another chance to prove how great the Super Duper fan really is. You might offer to replace the defective models (throwing in free shipping and delivery, of course) and include a 30 percent coupon for any other Super Duper product. You'd do it in a heartbeat, and not out of the goodness of your heart, not because you're a nice person, but because you care about your company and want everyone who does business with you to have a great experience.

Now explain this to me: if you care enough about your brand to react with this kind of interest and concern were you to overhear this conversation in person, why wouldn't you respond similarly if you read these same comments online? If there are conversations about your brand or your product or service category happening in coffee shops and beauty parlors and subways, they are most likely also happening on Facebook and Twitter and on all sorts of popular blogs and forums, and you can "hear" them all. These conversations were always happening before the advent of social media, of course, but there was only so far they could go. In addition, all a business could do if it became aware of these conversations was to eavesdrop. Now the talk and word of mouth about your company or brand can go on indefinitely, but you have a tremendous advantage the businesspeople before you didn't have: you and your entire team can participate in and propagate it. To ignore that option is to become a lonely fly on the wall—witness to everything that is said about you, powerless to do anything about it. All you're setting yourself up for is a face-to-face with a flyswatter.

Get on Board

If you're an entrepreneur, you surely already know I'm telling the truth because if you're having any success, it's extremely likely you're already engaging with your customers online and offline with equal intensity and enthusiasm. I hope my ideas and the examples in this book will inspire you to take your business to the next level, and give you ways to help others trying to make it.

If you want to become CEO one day, you absolutely have to get on board this train. Bringing about a massive cultural shift within a company takes a lot of time and finesse if you're going to do it well. You'll likely be competing against others who have been incorporating TYE principles into every aspect of how they do business from the day they opened their first Twitter account. The person who gets started the soonest has the advantage, though not because of the number of fans and followers they may have. I'm not sure what those people who promise to donate a thousand bucks to Haiti (if they can get a hundred people to follow them on Twitter) think they're accomplishing. Just give the thousand bucks to Haiti, you jerks! It's not the number of followers you have or "likes" you get, it's the strength of your bond with your followers that indicates how much anyone cares about what you have to say. In this game, the one with the most real relationships wins.

Mid-level managers who love what they do and want their company to compete and thrive and crush it have got to get this book onto their CEO's desk. Individuals can certainly adapt many of the lessons in this book to buff their own personal brand and even improve the way their department communicates and responds to the people and organizations with which they do business. But for a whole company to successfully enter the Thank You Economy, many small, practical steps and processes must be implemented that ultimately add up and result in a complete cultural transformation. Each baby step is easy to take, but only a total commitment to change over time from the top brass will ensure that the baby steps gain enough strength and speed to lead into a run. Unfortunately, many CEOs are afraid of implementing change, even when it's for the best long-term good of the company. That sounds harsh, but it's unfortunately true, and for good reason. I'm convinced that if company leaders didn't have to worry about stock prices or bonuses or their numbers, every one of them would be investing in social media by now. It just makes sense that the better you know your consumers, the better you can tailor your marketing to them, and the more likely they are to buy from you. But many leaders can't afford to worry about the long term, because their survival (and their bonus) depends on short-term results.

On a recent flight, I read an article by an editor-at-large for the *Harvard Business Review* (I know, I know, Mr. "I don't read anything" reads stuff from the *HBR* . . . insert your one-liner about me here) that perfectly crystallized the dilemma faced by even the most well-meaning CEOs: "Wall Street Is No Friend to Radical Innovation." The article reported the results of a study from the Wharton School that found that even when it was clear that an industry was about to be rocked by massive changes, Wall Street analysts primarily gave a thumbs-up to company strategies that relied on old technology, and seemed to ignore or minimize the validity of more daring attempts to take advantage of new technology. Wall Street puts CEOs in a near impossible situation, as described by Chris Trimble, on the faculty at Tuck School of Business at Dartmouth: "I've had CEOs tell me that ignoring Wall Street is the only way to do the right thing for the company's long-term future. They choose to invest in innovation, take the short-term punishment (in the form of a declining stock price), and hope that the punishment is not so severe that they lose their job." So what are people trying to convince their CEO that social media matters supposed to do when the metrics that they need to justify social media initiatives just aren't available yet?

Start. If you already have started, take a second look at what you're doing. Try on a new pair of glasses and reevaluate. Be prepared. Stay alert to new ideas and innovations. Do whatever you can to bring the Thank You Economy sensibility into your company, so that when you're finally able to implement initiatives, the foundation will already be set.

Companies can certainly survive without social media.

Maybe your competitors can afford to (over)spend on traditional platforms, or have a lot of brand equity built up thanks to amazing content. But if they do nothing with social media, and you do something, you will eventually have the potential to surpass them, not thanks to any one platform—and not overnight; it's a marathon, not a sprint—but because you acknowledge that culture and consumer expectations can and will change. That in and of itself means that you are more adaptable and flexible, and therefore have a better chance of surviving and flourishing in the Thank You Economy.

One more time: if you succeed with social media, it won't be because of the platform; it will be because you acknowledge that culture and consumer expectations can change. You are more adaptable and flexible than your competitors. If you apply social media correctly, your customers will buy more, they will be more loyal, they will spread your message, and they will defend you should you ever need them to. All of this adds up to your increased chance of surviving and flourishing in the Thank You Economy.

You know the business world has changed. You can feel it, can't you? Go to a shopping mall, a movie theater, a stadium, and look at what the masses are doing. For better or for worse, half if not more of the people are walking around with their heads down, their fingers sliding and tapping over their handheld devices.

Though girls ages fourteen to seventeen can still out-text anyone, averaging about a hundred texts per day compared to boys of the same age, who text about thirty times per day, texting isn't just for kids anymore. As of May 2010, 72 percent of the adult population were texting, at a rate of about ten texts per day. What do you think the number will look like by 2013?

When they're home, they've got those same handheld devices at their side, plus they're glued to their iPads and computers. Most of them are not just reading AOL's homepage anymore, I guarantee you. They're engaging with the content and their friends on Facebook and Twitter and Foursquare, Digg and Reddit, and a slew of websites you've probably never heard of. So why are you buying banner ads on AOL.com or Yahoo.com? Many of the brands that were relevant even five years ago no longer command respect or excitement because they've lost touch with their customers by continuing to talk to them almost exclusively via traditional marketing platforms. The customers aren't there in nearly the numbers they once were. They're on social media; you need to follow them, and talk to them, there. If you wait for your competitors to do this, and they do it right, they will steal any advantage you might have had right from under your nose.

For example, Zagat was the original consumer review destination, the "burgundy bible" for foodies, a twenty-year-old golden brand that never should have had to fight for relevance or survival. Yet because it was so slow to recognize that customer expectations and desires were changing, the company has had to roll up its sleeves and start swinging to defend itself. Zagat's story is a great example of how resistance to change and poor anticipation skills can hurt a giant in an industry. On the other hand, they're also an example of how companies can make a comeback once they figure out how to harness the innovation they once fumbled. To get a feel for the battle they've been waging, all you have to do is compare their timeline with those of one of their biggest competitors, Yelp.

1979: The Zagats hit upon the idea of collecting opinions from their friends and their friends' friends of New York City restaurants to create an informal yet reliable restaurant guide. Over the next two decades, *The Zagat Review* becomes an internationally recognized force in the culinary world, with over 100,000 contributing surveyors and a loyal readership.

1999: Zagat launches its website, but only paid subscribers can read full reviews.

2004: Former PayPal employees Jeremy Stoppelman and Russel Simmons launch Yelp from a San Francisco Mission Street office. The decidedly hip site offers free access to user reviews of restaurants, day spas, and other local businesses.

2007: Yelp reports five million unique visitors.

January 2008: The Zagats try to sell their business for $200 million. There are no takers.

May 2008: Yelp reports ten million unique visitors.

June 2008:	The Zagats take the business off the market.
July 2008:	Yelp releases the Yelp for iPhone app. The application is free.
November 2008:	Zagat releases the Zagat to Go iPhone app. It costs $10.
July 2009:	Zagat holds steady as one of the top ten iPhone apps in the travel category.
August 2009:	Yelp, which is still free, reports over 25 million unique visitors.
September 2009:	Zagat.com, which charges a $25 annual membership fee, gets about 270,000 unique visitors per month, and is "trending downward."
December 2009:	Yelp turns down a $550 million offer from Google, and a $700 million offer from Microsoft. "Yelp has the chance to become one of the great Internet brands," says Stoppelman. "That for me is the chance of a lifetime."
January 2010:	Modeling Foursquare, Yelp adds a "check in" feature to its app upgrade.
February 2010:	Zagat teams up with Foursquare. Foursquare users can earn a "Foodie" badge when they check in to Zagat-rated restaurants, and receive menu recommendations from the Zagat collection of reviews.
August 2010:	Zagat is ranked the most-followed brand on Foursquare by Osnapz, with 65,000 followers.
August 2010:	Zagat integrates Foodspotting, which al-

lows people to post photos and comment about the foods they love rather than read and write full-blown reviews, into the Zagat To Go app.

If Zagat had kept an eye on the innovation horizon, Yelp never would have been able to cut into their market share in the first place. Yet as you can see, Zagat has swung hard and gotten in a few good hits. It is possible for brands, websites, and new businesses to take market share from sleeping giants, and even become market leaders, but if the sleeping giant awakens and uses the brand equity it has created over the years, it can absolutely get back in the game. This is good news for any larger organization that is only now recognizing that it needs to make social media a priority. Ideally, however, any giants who are awakening will adjust because they understand what is happening around them and want to adjust, not because, like Zagat, they have been backed into a corner and have no other choice.

It's Not About Social Media

As I said in *Crush It!*,

Social Media = Business

The thing to keep in mind at all costs, though, is that the Thank You Economy is much, much bigger than social media. Social media's arrival was simply the catalyst for a revolution that was already brewing in the minds of consumers sick to death of feeling isolated, unappreciated, and ignored. *The Thank*

You Economy explains how businesses must learn to adapt their marketing strategies to take advantage of platforms that have completely transformed consumer culture and society as a whole. If this were 1923, this book would have been called *Why Radio Is Going to Change the Game.* If it were 1995, it would be *Why Amazon Is Going to Take Over the Retailing World.* I'm not proposing an all-or-nothing approach—there is still a place for brick-and-mortar businesses in a world where Amazon exists, and traditional media is still relevant and valuable. (Probably didn't think I'd say that, huh? Wait till you read chapter five.) But there are too many businesses that are still holding back, watching the social media train rush by, convinced that if the destination is so great, another train will come along soon enough. They seem to think that it will be going more slowly, and the ride will be safe and steady, and they'll be able to catch up with everyone else who jumped on early. They're wrong, though. The next train, when it shows up, will be going full speed to some other equally exotic and unknown place. Social media is here to stay, but eventually, some technological innovation will be invented that will give intrepid travelers, the ones who understand that these trains of change are the only trains coming, another chance to move way ahead of the risk-averse. (I think anyone paying attention can see that mobile platforms are the next key to picking up market share . . . please tell me that you have a mobile strategy . . .) What will not change, however, is the culture—the expectation—of communication, transparency, and connection that social media revived. We live in a world where anyone with a computer can have an online presence and a voice; whatever follows next will simply make the power of word of mouth that much more powerful. The proliferation of blogs, with their invitation to comment, and the transparency of Facebook and Twitter, has marked an economic turning point. People thought they had seen a massive cultural shift when the public adopted the Internet into their daily lives, but the bigger shift occurred when the Internet began to allow for two-way conversation. Learn how to implement a culture of caring and communication into your business, scale your one-to-one relationships, and watch your customers reward your efforts by using their new and massively powerful word of mouth to market your business and your brand for you.

CHAPTER TWO

Erasing Lines in the Sand

I n 1997, shortly after I launched WineLibrary.com, I was invited to a conference hosted by a local chapter of the New Jersey Chamber of Commerce to talk about online selling. It was my first speaking engagement, and I was pumped. I sat in the wings, trying to stay calm, as the speaker before me walked out onstage. He wore a tie. He had VP credentials and a fancy PowerPoint presentation. And the theme of his talk was that dotcom retail was a crock. It wasn't practical, and it would never take off because, as the data on his PowerPoint slides revealed, nobody in Middle America was buying, nor would they ever buy, on the Internet. Mr. PowerPoint asked the audience, "How many of you have heard of Amazon?" A solid number of people raised their hands. He went on to ask if they really thought people would abandon the relationships they'd built over the years with their local bookstores, or even bypass super-stocked Barnes & Noble. They didn't. It would be another two years before CEO Jeff Bezos would be named *Time*'s Person of the Year, his name underscored on the cover by the subhead "E-commerce is changing the way the world shops." It would be another four years before Amazon reached its first quarterly net profit. Mr. PowerPoint compared the company's rising market share to its nonexistent profits and said that one day we would all look back and say, "Remember Amazon?"

My short-term dream at the time was to become the Amazon for wine, and the audience I was about to explain that dream to was staring at this PowerPointing clown's charts and graphs as if they were carved stone tablets brought down by Moses. As he finished up, he said, "This kid's now going to tell you how he's going to sell wine on the Internet. How many of you here would ever buy wine on the Internet?" Only one or two people out of sixty or seventy raised their hands.

You know if this had happened in 2010, the talk would have been recorded and I could have posted it to show everyone what a jerk he was. But believe it or not, even though he called me a kid, he did earn my respect for calling me out. I like people with competitive spirit and bravado; they bring out the fight in me. Not that I won any battles that day. I walked out onstage and opened my talk by saying, "With all due respect to Mr. PowerPoint, he has no idea what he's talking about. He is going to be on the wrong side of history. I feel bad for him." I went on to tell my story, and gave my audience my best, most heartfelt argument as to why the Internet would be to retailers what the printing press was to writers. To the end, they remained a very skeptical, uninterested crowd.

Entrepreneurs have a sort of sixth sense that tells them when big change is afoot. The *Time* magazine article that accompanied Bezos's Person of the Year award describes it best:

Every time a seismic shift takes place in our economy, there are people who feel the vibrations long before the rest of us do, vibrations so strong they demand action—action that can seem rash, even stupid. Ferry owner Cornelius Vanderbilt jumped ship when he saw the railroads coming. Thomas Watson Jr., overwhelmed by his sense that computers would be everywhere even when they were nowhere, bet his father's office-machine company on it: IBM.

Jeffrey Preston Bezos had that same experience when he first peered into the maze of connected computers called the World Wide Web and realized that the future of retailing was glowing back at him.

Looking back, I can't hold Mr. PowerPoint's skepticism against him, nor can I blame the audience for dismissing most of what I had to say. Most people's DNA simply doesn't allow them an entrepreneur's anticipation skills. They don't see potential in the unknown, they see a threat to their comfort zone, so their knee-jerk reaction is to draw a deep line in the sand between themselves and anything new or unproven, especially when it comes to technology. Close to 90 percent of Americans own cell phones, but people my age can still remember when many questioned the need to be, and even the wisdom of being, reachable by phone at any time. Just four short years ago, we actually used those phones for talking, not texting. And no one was playing Farmville on Facebook.* How many of today's more than 500 million Facebook users swore

---

* If you're reading this and it's 2014, could you email me how much actual money you're spending on virtual goods?

they'd never use the site?* There's a reason the divide between innovators—people who eagerly embrace new technology—and the majority has been described as a chasm.

Most businesspeople spend far too long on the wrong side of that chasm, hiding behind tired sayings like "You can only manage what you measure." That's how my nemesis won back in 1997. He had numbers from sources the audience trusted; any numbers I might have been able to point to came from research that still hadn't made its way to the mainstream. No matter how strongly I could feel the vibrations of the future, without hard numbers from old-school sources indicating that the Internet was going to change how Americans thought about buying and selling everything from books and wine to toilet paper and asparagus, I couldn't win over the corporate mindset.

Corporate America loves ecommerce now, of course, but business leaders and brand managers and marketers have simply drawn new lines in the sand, this time putting distance between their companies and social media, all the while desperately clinging to the security they still believe numbers can provide. Unfortunately, if you wait until social media is able to prove itself to you before deciding to engage with your customers one-on-one, you'll have missed your greatest window of opportunity to move ahead of your competitors.

---

* You know, I don't think I want that to be a rhetorical question. If you were one of those people, I'd love to know. Email me and confess at gary@vaynermedia.com.

Resistance Won't Kill You Right Away

What should the horse-and-buggy driver have done when he noticed the automobile? Should he have waited until he was down to three fares per day to consider that maybe he needed to make a change in how he was going to make a living, or should he have quickly sold the horses? Sell the frigging horses, of course! Company leaders may not see their lack of participation in social media reflected on their P&L statement, but I promise that, unless something else sinks their company first, they will. Just because you ignore a threat doesn't mean it doesn't exist. Will you die if you smoke? Not necessarily. Not everyone who smokes dies of lung cancer, and if smokers live long enough, there are plenty of other things that can kill them. Likewise, you're not going out of business tomorrow if you're not on Facebook and Twitter and blogging and creating content and building community. But the risk that your business will die before its time grows bigger every day that you don't use social media. You think Barnes & Noble and Borders didn't see Amazon coming in 1997? Of course they did. But the numbers distracted them, and the numbers said that Amazon was nowhere near making a profit, and Barnes & Noble and Borders were still the number-one-and-two book retailers in the country. Even if some Borders and Barnes & Noble execs could sense that change was coming, they probably preferred to believe the story the numbers told them. To doubt the numbers would have meant revamping and hustling like crazy, and it is so much easier to do things the way they've always been done before. B. Dalton, owned by Barnes & Noble, didn't go out of business in 1999. It didn't happen in 2001, or even 2003. It didn't happen until January 2010, when the last store finally closed. But it did finally happen, and it didn't have to. Like the guy who quits smoking only after being diagnosed with lung cancer, by the time B. Dalton realized that Amazon was a force to be reckoned with, it was too late.

No big company loses to a little company if they are totally committed to winning the fight. There is no reason why mammoth companies like Barnes & Noble or Borders could not have spent real money and hired the right people to come at Amazon with everything they had. Barnes & Noble went online in 1997, but they didn't go in 100 percent; they couldn't have, or Amazon wouldn't have taken over so much of their market. They should have done the same thing I do every time a new liquor store that could be a threat opens up near me—pound the competitor's face in with advertising and marketing dollars (even if they're not opening up close to me, you can bet I'm paying close attention to what they're doing). Barnes & Noble should have come at Amazon the way Fox and NBC came at Google, when they developed a true rival, Hulu, to combat Google's YouTube.

Right now, I'd say that social media is a bit like a kidney—you can survive with only one, but your chances of making it to old age are a lot better with two. Eventually, though, I think social media will be as important to a business as a strong heart.

CHAPTER THREE

Why Smart People Dismiss Social Media, and Why They Shouldn't

've talked to a lot of corporations about the benefits of social media over the last six years, and most of the reasons I've heard as to why leaders don't want to invest in it hinge on fear. As I've discussed, Wall Street doesn't make it easy for companies to take many risks. Maybe there was some risk in the early days, but at this point the risk anyone is avoiding exists only in his or her own head. I know that can be hard to believe when you're staring at headlines that read "Most Brands Still Irrelevant on Twitter," and "Social Networking May Not Be as Profitable as Many Think." It's possible that for now those headlines and others like them are technically true, but if they are, in almost every case, the reason is the same—most of the companies already attempting to use social media platforms aren't using them correctly. I mean, just because you can't dribble well or get the rock in the hoop doesn't mean that there's a design flaw in your basketball. And the reason they're not using them correctly is generally because they aren't fully committed to it; they still don't get that intent matters. It is true that you need to use social media because otherwise your competitors will get ahead of you. Yet how we speak and behave when we're going through the motions of caring is vastly different from how we speak and behave when we care from the bottom of our hearts. Our intent affects the force of our actions, so if a leader has simply got a case of monkey see, monkey do (where people throw themselves and their companies into social media solely because their competitor is doing it) and her intent isn't to infuse every aspect of her business with Thank You Economy principles, of course she'll never reap the full benefits. She's like a competitive swimmer who hangs around the edge of the pool for a month, carefully dipping her toes and analyzing the water, and who then complains that her swim times aren't improving.

Overall, there are eleven excuses I've heard companies use again and again to justify their refusal to fully commit to and invest in social media, and I want to dissect them all. If you're a skeptic, I hope you'll find some new information here that will persuade you that the time to act has come. If you are eager to get your company to connect on a deeper level with its customers but are meeting with resistance, I hope these pages will provide fresh talking points and facts you can use when presenting this issue to the heads of your company or department. One thing is absolutely certain—until leaders erase this particular line in the sand, they will be severely hampered in their attempts to guide their companies smoothly and successfully into the Thank You Economy.

1. There's no ROI.

Brand managers and company leaders are obsessed with numbers because the numbers matter a great deal, if not to them personally, then to their superiors, their stockholders, and the financial and business media. I get that. But let me ask this: what is the return on investment for any kind of customer caring? Is there a formula that calculates how many positive interactions it takes to pay off in a sale or in a recommendation? No, but until now good managers and salespeople have killed their customers with kindness anyway, because even without hard numbers to quantify the ROI, they instinctively know that earning a customer's trust is key.

Now, Nielsen has numbers that prove the link between generating trust and making a sale isn't just theoretical. When Nielsen conducted a study on what drives consumer trust, the results were clear: almost 70 percent of people turn to *family and friends* for advice when making purchasing decisions. Where have people been talking to their family and friends lately? Facebook reports that 60 percent of the people online are going to social networks, with half returning every day. If there is ROI in friendship and family, there has to be ROI in social media. "We often forget the symbiotic relationship between trust and ROI," says Pete Blackshaw of NM Incite, a joint venture of McKinsey and Nielsen, and also author of *Satisfied Customers Tell Three Friends, Angry Customers Tell 3000*. "If consumers trust other consumers more than they trust traditional advertising, and the platforms to convey their trusted recommendations are now reaching billions, the ROI should start to enter the 'no brainer' zone. There's clearly nuance in the executional elements, and some social media techniques or tactics will clearly drive more ROI than others, but the big picture should be obvious."

When faced with two equal choices, people often buy for no other reason than they associate one choice with someone they know. My friends shop at Wine Library, and they go out of their way to do so. Most of my acquaintances from high school shop at Wine Library, too. There is a Dell consumer out there who buys Dell because he has an uncle who works there. There are plenty of people who never stopped buying their gas at Exxon after the Valdez spill, or more recently, from BP, even though they were upset by the environmental catastrophes those companies caused, because they have friends or relatives connected to them. Social media, which allows people to see their family and friends' preferences and interactions with brands, allows for many more chances for people to make the personal associations that can lead to buying decisions.

The ROI of a company's engagement with a customer scales in proportion to the bonds of the relationship. The ROI of your relationship with your mother is going to be much higher than that of the one you have with a good friend. Both, however, are more valuable than the one you have with an acquaintance, which trumps the relationship you have with a stranger. Without social media, you and your customer are relegated to strangers; with it, depending on your efforts, you can potentially upgrade your relationship to that of casual acquaintances, and even, in time, to friends. The power of that relationship can go so far as to convert a casual browser into a committed buyer, or a buyer into an advocate.

Every company should be bending over backward to transform customers into advocates—they are incredibly valuable. According to an IBM study of online retail consumer buying patterns:

- Advocates' share of wallet is 33 percent more than that of customers who aren't advocates.
- Advocates spend about 30 percent more dollars with their favorite online retailers than non-advocates do.
- Advocates stick around longer, proving themselves less likely than other customers to switch to a competitor even if it offers similar products at similar prices.
- Advocates have significantly higher lifetime value than regular customers, for not only do they spend more now, they are more likely to keep spending, and even increase their spending, as time goes on.

Advocates are bred, not born. According to Nielsen, consumers are generally more motivated to reach out to a company with a complaint than with praise. However, they are willing to publicly praise a company when given the opportunity to do so. Social media allows companies to provide ample prompts for consumers to remember why they like a brand, and inspire them to say so publicly, whether on the company website or via social networking channels. Through an exhaustive consumer-engagement study that focused on moms online, Pete Blackshaw found that when brands started investing in meaningful interactions and conversations with mothers, the mothers were 30 percent more likely to become advocates. In other words, they were willing to write favorable online reviews about the product, essentially doing the brand's marketing for it. According to Blackshaw, marketers consider online reviews among the most coveted form of consumer expression, because they tend to show up close to the "purchase event," and because their clicks and links result in higher search results. The study showed, in addition, that mothers who became "high participator moms"— answering questions from other mothers, providing information, and creating online content about the product or brand— saved the brands 15 percent on call support. Overall, the numbers show that there is significant ROI in engaging with customers and strengthening your relationship with them. Blackshaw, who has consulted with hundreds of Fortune 1000 brands, says this is especially true in the early phase of a new product launch. "The early reviews can be as impactful as a $10 million media buy in shaping early perceptions, even among the traditional media, who increasingly lean on social media as a 'cheat sheet' to understand what's *really* going on with brands."

Even if only a small percentage of your customers become true advocates, there is tremendous ROI in treating your customers as well as possible. According to Jason Mittelstaedt, chief marketing officer of RightNow, a customer service consulting firm that published the Customer Service Impact 2010 Report, *85 percent of U.S. consumers say they would pay 5 percent to 25 percent more to ensure a superior customer experience.* In addition, 76 percent of consumers say they appreciate it when brands and companies take a personal interest in them. In other words, advocates and non-advocates alike say they want superior service, and they're willing to pay for it. Can there be any doubt that engaging one-on-one with customers, making each and every one feel valued and heard, constitutes a superior experience?

Consider these statistics pulled from the Customer Experience Impact 2010 Report as well:

- 40 percent of consumers switched to buying from a competitor because of its reputation for great customer service.
- 55 percent cite great service, not product or price, as their primary reason for recommending a company.
- 66 percent said that great customer service was their primary driver for greater spending.

It's very logical: There is proven ROI in doing whatever you can to turn your customers into advocates for your brand or business. The way to create advocates is to offer superior customer service. In the Thank You Economy, a key component of superior customer service is one-to-one engagement in social media. It's what customers want, and as we all know, the customer is king.

2. The metrics aren't reliable.

The tools for tracking and measuring social media initiatives are becoming increasingly sophisticated and reliable. After all, this data is coming from Nielsen. If you place television ads, you've probably been making enormous financial decisions based on the Nielsen ratings for years, trusting them to tell networks who is watching what shows so the networks and cable stations can charge you a fortune to place your brand in your target demographics' line of sight. And by the time you're reading this book, you'll be able to rely on metrics bearing the Nielsen seal of approval for your online ads, as well. In September 2010, Nielsen announced that it was launching a cross-media metrics tool that will measure a campaign's effectiveness online, with ratings data comparable to that already offered for TV. One of its first partners to test the new tool? Facebook. In the press release, Steve Hasker, Nielsen's president of Media Products, said, "This new system will provide marketers with a better understanding of their ROI, and will give media companies a much needed tool to prove the value of their audiences."

But what about engagement? The new tool from Nielsen measures the effect of online ads, not whether all that time a company spends talking to customers online translates to sales. Well, in 1990, how many execs imagined they'd be spending money to post banner ads on that thing called the Internet? Placing product in video games? It was unthinkable. How about paying for SEO? SEO, what the heck is that? Now, you put a lot of money into SEO.*

---

* You might want to rethink that money you're putting into SEO, by the way. I'm not a huge fan of SEO, and I think its value as a brand awareness tool is going to weaken as platforms develop that leverage the relationship between a business or brand and an information seeker. Remember the kid I watched in Best Buy who used a status update to get the information he needed from his friends to pick a video game.

Everything we count on today to tell us how our marketing efforts are working was once brand-new and risky. And then it wasn't. So it will be with social media and the metrics that accompany it.

In 2010, *Ad Week* reported that Vitrue, a social media management company, had calculated that a million Facebook fans were worth $3.6 million in "equivalent media" over a year; $3.60 per person interested enough in your brand to friend you up is not chump change. If that number had come from Nielsen, everyone in the marketing and advertising industry would have treated it as gospel. The metrics already in existence are being refined with incredible speed, and the fixed standards execs crave so much are on their way.

Will there still be ways for consumers to game the system? Of course. But the vast majority of people on Facebook and Twitter are actually living within the medium. If they're not there, the conversation stops. If they get distracted or lose interest, the conversation changes. The data businesses can collect about what their customers are talking about, with whom they're talking about it, and how often, is far less ambiguous than it's ever been. The problems in accurately measuring impressions that plague traditional media will continue for online ads, but the data about consumers' experience and their perception of your brand is right there to collect with every tweet, button, heart symbol, comment, and share. Even better, by engaging one-on-one, you can ask for clarification, request details, and really delve into why your customer feels the way he or she does.

Every media platform has loopholes. When I first suggested buying Google ads, my father wasn't convinced it was a good idea. How would we know that real people had clicked through?

What if it was just our competitors making us think the ads were working and driving up our budget? Well, I didn't know. But I was pretty sure that my competitors were too busy with their own marketing to spend the kind of time it would take to sabotage mine. Google claimed to have an algorithm to prevent fraud, and it seemed to me it was in Google's best interest to protect me. Believe me, I wasn't in business to lose money. But I was thinking long term, and long-term thinking requires that you look at all the options, including the ones that might take a little time to pay off. All media-buying decisions are based on best educated guesses, so it makes no sense for people to hesitate to use a new tool, especially one with such a low cost of entry.

3. Social media is still too young.

The wait-and-see approach, the one most companies have used while considering when to invest in traditional platforms, won't work for social media. First-to-market in this hyper-fast world has impact. Companies can no longer just spend money and get in on the game. Before, it wouldn't have mattered if, hypothetically, Nike (which wasn't founded until the mid-1970s) had taken one look at the radio when it was first invented and said, "Cripes, this is going to be big, it's going to be in cars!" and gotten a $3 million head start over Adidas. Six years later, once Adidas had looked around and said, "Darn, Nike was right!" and pounded the platform with a $4 million campaign, it would have been even with, if not ahead of, Nike. All Adidas would have had to do was spend a lot of money to push its message out and the consumer would have swallowed it, because there was so much of it they could hardly see anything else. It could have trumped the other company's longer presence on the platform with volume, a push platform. Companies can't buy volume in social media, though, so today, those six years Nike would have had on Adidas would count a great deal, because those are six years that Nike would have been going into the trenches, talking to people and inviting them to talk back, creating an emotional bond and solidifying its relationship with the consumer. Adidas wouldn't be able to come out of nowhere and magically create relationships where there aren't any, and it would have a hard time pulling customers away from Nike because they would be emotionally attached.

Adidas would not be locked out, though. If its leaders channeled their efforts in the right direction and created a campaign that really communicated with people and made consumers feel as though Adidas cared more about them and their business than Nike did, they could still close that emotional gap. It could take a little while, but it would definitely be doable.

For once, I'm begging businesses to take the easier path. Embarking on one-to-one customer engagement offers significant long-term rewards, but the company will also experience immediate benefits—greater brand awareness, stronger brand loyalty, increased word of mouth, improved understanding of customer needs, and better, faster consumer feedback—and suffer very few drawbacks, if any. Meanwhile, the drawback to resisting social media engagement is clear: the longer you wait, the farther the competition can pull ahead.

Jumping on social media platforms early gives you a tremendous advantage, because people are more engaged early on as they explore all the possibilities of the medium; there's more chatter, more overall usage, and less noise to break through. You don't have to shout and turn cartwheels to be heard. Being first on the scene is not all that counts, and you can certainly catch up later, but your cost of entry will be significantly higher, and you will work considerably harder.

The kind of impression you're trying to make can't be bought the way it could on the traditional media platforms. This isn't just about hitting someone with an image so many times it sears your brand name into the person's brain. It's about building relationships, and relationships take time. The twelve months you wait to get in on this is twelve months that your competitor will have spent connecting and building goodwill and trust with customers who could have been your customers. On this platform, it's not just the thirty or sixty seconds of a well-placed spot that have value—all time has value, just as it does in the real world.

During my first three and a half years of high school, I was so consumed by my baseball card business and my job at Wine Library, which was then called Shopper's Discount Liquors, I hardly ever socialized with my classmates. Then, around spring break of senior year, I realized that I was about to miss out, and that I had one last chance to make up for it. So I threw myself into the social scene. I have an outgoing personality and a good sense of humor, and I became more popular pretty quickly. But do I have the same connection to high school friends as classmates who invested all four years into building relationships with each other? Absolutely not. Real, lasting friendships take emotional investment, and I took too long to decide to invest.

Social media relationships and personal relationships work exactly the same way—you get out of them what you put into them. You can't buy them, force them, or make them into something they're not ready to be.

The longer you hesitate to build a presence on this platform, the more you will struggle to make it work for you. That's why so many brands, especially celebrity brands, are having a hard time with it. Many big names are not jumping onto Twitter and Facebook because they fear that if they do it now, they could hurt their brand more than help it. What if they launch and their numbers aren't impressive? What if they don't attract the huge flock of followers or fans they think they have?* Though as I keep repeating, the number of people with whom you have connections is far less important than the quality of those connections, it's just a fact that most of the world looks at those numbers and judges you for them. Low numbers could hurt a brand. If this platform worked like TV or radio, a celebrity or an established brand might just buy someone else's fan base to make themselves look better, much the way companies buy up smaller companies or databases. But that's just it; this platform doesn't work at all like yesterday's platforms. Even if you could take over someone else's fan base to boost your numbers, those numbers exist only because of the relationship that's been built, a relationship entirely dependent upon a sustained authentic interaction between brand and customer. Rihanna can't buy Kanye West's fans; Blue Bell can't buy Ben and Jerry's fans. Amazon can buy Zappos, but

---

* The only people who have to fear low numbers are those who have artificially inflated their value and popularity.

it can't buy Zappos' fans. Amazon could do what many acquirers do—fold the newly acquired company into the parent company, adapt the Zappos business processes to match their own, take over the Zappos warehouses, suck all the soul out of it and leave nothing intact but the logo. Amazon would have the customers, sure, but it would not have the customer relationships. If Zappos were no longer the Zappos they knew and loved, the customers would abandon ship, and ultimately Amazon would gain nothing from the acquisition. Fortunately, Amazon gets that the key to Zappos' success is to leave it alone and keep its soul intact, so it will probably reap the benefits it was looking to buy.

You can catch the leader in your space only if you get in the pool. So what if some people notice your numbers are a little low? I believe we're dawning on an era when more people will recognize the value of quality over quantity, but until then, the effect of low numbers on your brand will feel like a bee sting compared to the hemorrhaging gunshot wound it will feel like if you do nothing. Get in, and then start swimming better and faster than anyone else. You do this by being more genuine and more caring, by creating better content, by keeping your thumb on the pulse of the space, and by being more engaged. By being better. You have to act like the guy who falls for the girl who just got dumped by the love of her life. How the heck are you going to get her to let him go, and make her see that you're worth ten of that dude? With an unbelievable amount of patience, persistence, and understanding. Do it right, with genuine feeling, and there's a chance that one day she'll look at you the same way she used to look at him.

People want to have close relationships with their brands. It still sounds a little weird today, but one day it won't. The right time to start building those relationships is right now.

4. Social media is just another trend that will pass.

One reason why business and marketing leaders may be slow to accept social media is that for all the talk about how fast the business world is always changing and how speed is of the essence, platforms have historically remained remarkably steady. Newspapers and magazines have been luring us with attention-grabbing headlines and alluring pictures for hundreds of years. It wasn't until 1922 that radio gave companies a new platform with which to experiment, and then businesses had to wait more than two decades before TV gave them another opportunity in the late 1940s and '50s. After that, forty years went by before the Internet arrived.

Given how spoiled they've been by the predictability and stability of the one-way platforms they're used to, it's no surprise that most business and marketing leaders have been skeptical about the viability of social media as the next big one. But there's a saying in the NFL: speed kills. Ten years ago, a five-foot-eight, 180-pound player would never have been drafted. Now, a really short, shifty, fast running back like Noel Devine can go into the first round. That's how much the league has changed in a decade, and it has totally changed the game. Social media has changed the game in even less time, making levels of communication that would have been unthinkable ten years ago the norm today. The growth and technological shifts we are experiencing today have a faster and greater impact on business than they used to. You can't expect any product's penetration to follow the same pattern that, say, the Walkman did thirty years ago.

Some marketing planners don't dismiss the idea of social media so much as they mistrust the sticking power of any particular platform. After all, in 2006 MySpace was hot, and within three years Facebook had overtaken it in terms of users and engagement. Why wouldn't Facebook suffer the same fate when the next hot platform comes along? Well, if it's not as good as the new thing, it will suffer the same fate as MySpace (though it should be noted that MySpace is not anywhere near dead yet, attracting 65 million unique users in September 2010, according to the market research company comScore). But it wouldn't matter. If users one day abandon Facebook in favor of something better, they won't be jumping off the train, they'll simply be moving to a new car. Move with them. The relationships you've worked to build won't evaporate so long as you follow your customers and keep up the caring. There have been plenty of lifelong friendships that started when someone from New York met someone from Florida while vacationing in Las Vegas. Before social media, they exchanged phone calls, and sent letters and holiday cards. Now they friend each other up. What happened in Vegas never has to stay in Vegas unless you choose to let the relationships you begin there die.

5. We need to control our message.

I would love to see that companies have recognized the stupidity of this argument by the time this book is in print, but I have a funny feeling many still won't. A lot of companies resist building a Facebook wall, blogging, or starting a Twitter or YouTube account because an irate customer might post negative comments. So what? Would you prefer that the customer post them somewhere else where you have absolutely no way to reply? Or somewhere you can't even find? If you're that afraid of your customer, you might want to take a closer look at how you're doing business.

You can't control the message; that ship has sailed. Yes, things can go crazy-mad online, and companies have suffered from out-of-control negative word of mouth. But it's highly unlikely that when companies sink under the weight of a mistake, it was entirely because of that mistake. If they folded, it was because there was something fundamentally wrong with the business model or with management that resulted in too many repeated problems. The one that brought the company to its knees wasn't the only straw, just the final one that broke its back.

Small or midsize companies might fear that they wouldn't survive a big faux pas the way a juggernaut might—like Tylenol, which suffered a blow almost thirty years ago when someone put cyanide in its pills and placed contaminated bottles back in stores—but they needn't worry.

Overall, problems can be fixed if you catch them in time. If you plead your case quickly and sincerely, you'll gain back the customers' trust, as Ann Taylor did. When Ann Taylor LOFT introduced their silk cargo pants on their Facebook page in the summer of 2010, a wave of online customers complained that no one except a giraffe-sized, skinny model could possibly look good in them. To prove them wrong, LOFT employees of all heights and sizes posted photos of themselves wearing the pants. The response was extraordinary: tons of comments from women thanking LOFT for listening, some even admitting that they might wear the pants. This customer couldn't be swayed, but her comment illustrates why it is in a brand's best interest to nurture customer relationships:

> I love LOFT and I sooooo appreciate you taking the time to "listen" to our comments and show these pants on "real" women. I hope you will continue to do this in the future. However, I still maintain these pants are UGLY. They dont even look like capris on #2. I did want to say thank you though and to let you know I shop at Loft, but these pants are FAIL. ;)

The customer still hates the pants, but now LOFT knows they've still got their evangelist out there, and there's a good chance that she's spreading the word.

When I first started working for my dad, any time a customer called or came to the store to complain, it would ruin his life. The man would go red in the face, he would get upset, he'd just want to go home. He was just crushed, which is a great testament to how much my father cared about his customers (and I respect and love him so much for being that way). I, on the other hand, was ecstatic when one of these unhappy customers called, because now that I knew there was a problem, I could try to fix it. I would spend the rest of my life fixing things for that customer if I had to. And it always worked, even when dealing with some of the toughest SOBs I have ever met. More than once I had to go to someone's home and orchestrate a dinner and pour the wine—all for free.

In this case, the cost of what I put into getting that customer back was rarely close to the yearly, maybe even lifetime, value of the customer (which is, by the way, the huge advantage that companies that aren't trying to hit quarterly numbers have over publicly held companies). But I was creating a culture, and I was establishing my brand. I wanted my employees to absorb my vibe and mission, and layer it over everything they did. It's possible that I lost eight hundred bucks bringing a particularly difficult customer back into the fold. But every time I did something like that, I won, because I was strengthening the DNA of my employees and my company, which paid off in the long run.

I would never put myself out of business, so I lost only what I knew I could afford to lose. Anyone can scale that kind of service and attention. What's great is that now it's far cheaper to cater to your customers this way than it used to be. Back then I had to go to someone's house and pair wines with food for dinner, which kept my efforts local. Now I can make a personalized video on YouTube for free and send it to anyone, anywhere, with a bottle of wine or a $100 credit. There are so many more channels we can now use to communicate our good intent directly to our customers, with a personal, individually customized message that is impossible to achieve through TV or print.

You can fix anything unless you're doing something grossly wrong. If you're putting rat poison in your pickles or using child labor, no matter how cheap or convenient you are compared to your competitor, you're eventually going to lose. But if the only issue for the pickle company is that the new lid is too hard to twist off, or the new and improved flavor of your dill pickles is making people gag, you can do something about that.

I suspect that even BP has a prayer, and their screwup in the Gulf is one of the worst man-made environmental disasters we've ever seen. People were pissed off at Exxon for a while back in the 1980s, too—remember, when the *Valdez* ran aground and sprung a leak off the coast of Alaska? Exxon took a hit, but it's not hard to find one of their gas stations almost anywhere in the country, even though there have always been plenty of other oil companies people could choose to buy from to refuel their cars. Tylenol is still going strong almost three decades after its cyanide scare, and it will certainly survive the two recalls it announced in 2010. People still go to see Hugh Grant movies. Over time, if a company or brand handles its disaster management plan properly, most people will forget, and even forgive.

Business leaders consistently underestimate two things. First, they underestimate people's willingness to forgive. They are afraid to put up fan pages because they think any negative comment is equal to a *60 Minutes* private investigation showing the whole world how much they stink. Very rarely is that the case, and if you are honest with your fans, followers, and customers, and allow them to see exactly what steps you are taking to make things right, the only feature *60 Minutes* will be interested in doing on you will be for your savvy social media skills.

Second, they underestimate people's bullshit radar. That's why it never works when a brand launches an effort that effectively tries to trick people to retweet, like a "Fan me up and I'll donate to Haiti" campaign, or tries to make something go viral. You can't make something go viral. All you can do is put out fantastic content. If it's that good, it will go viral all on its own. (And I'll say it again: just donate to Haiti and shut up!)

The best thing you can do for your brand and your company is to make sure that you put the truth out there for anyone who wants to hear it. You want negative comments to show up on your fan page. The person who posts a negative comment is a customer you can talk to. The customer you should be scared of is the one who has a bad experience, doesn't say a word, and never returns. Thinking about that person should keep you up at night. You have no idea how to get the person back, and you might not even realize that you've lost a customer. The person who says to you on Twitter, "I bleeping hate you!" is an awesome customer to have. If you can give alienated customers what they want, they will come back to you stronger than ever. Every time.

Giving people what they want doesn't translate to caving every time someone makes an unreasonable demand or threatens to tweet out something ugly. You have to listen to your customers, but you don't have to do what they tell you to do. Even if you can't satisfy every desire, you can make it clear that you wish you could. You can express regret that someone is dissatisfied with the outcome of your exchange. You can try to offer an alternative. (For a model example of how a CEO should talk to an unhappy customer, see the email note from John Pepper of Boloco, on page 97.) Many times people lash out because they feel as though it's the only way to get some attention—the squeaky wheel gets the grease, after all.* Hear them, make the call, and

---

* The excessive attention we pay to squeaky wheels is contributing to a lot of misses right now. I know I was guilty of doing it when I was getting started with social media. We need to make sure that we focus on the emerging advocates for our brands, especially micro-celebrities, and not get overwhelmed by the small percentage of problems we sometimes have to handle.

explain why you made it. As long as you always take the high road, you will minimize the impact of their dissatisfaction on your business. Negativity launched online out of spite will be easily spotted as such if you keep your own tone polite and your message clear and consistent. Don't bother to get into a debate, even if you're right. It's not worth the effort, and again, you won't win.

The best problem you can have is offering such great service that you wind up spoiling your customers. Mine expect a tremendous amount from me, as well they should. Sometimes they ask for too much, and when they do, I address it. For example, some of my local clients recently informed me that they were annoyed that Wine Library would offer free shipping on our sister site Cinderellawine.com because it means nonlocals can get a better deal on it. But I explained to them, you get the store. The customers in San Francisco (who sometimes buy a lot more than the locals) don't get to attend the free wine tastings, they can't stop by anytime to see what's new or talk to my staff, and they can't nibble on the free cheese samples and other goodies we make available. I firmly believe that all the perks balance out and that everyone who shops with me gets a great deal. After I explained my position, some of my local customers saw my point, and the issue was resolved. Not everyone was satisfied with my answer, but I am certain everyone appreciated the fact that I made an effort to respond in as much detail as possible. I treated the dissatisfied people the way they should have been treated—like valuable customers!

Had they wanted to, they could have badmouthed me or my store all over Facebook and Twitter. But they didn't, because I kept the conversation civil and honest. And if they had, I wouldn't have worried too much about it. What's brilliant about social media platforms is that no matter what someone else chooses to say about you, you can put the facts out there, on your fan page, on your blog, and in your tweets. People can track events and dialogue as they unfold. Everyone can see the exchange and make his or her own judgment call. As long as you stay on message, and remain honest, polite, and as accommodating as possible, you'll have nothing to fear from someone with a grudge. Good manners are about treating your customers with respect at all times. You may not be able to control the message anymore, but you can absolutely control the tone in which the message gets played.

Controlling their message and their image explains why so many—too many—companies still refuse to allow their employees to publicly blog and tweet about their work. I understand their fear, but it's unwarranted. In fact, there might be no better way to know for sure that you're making smart hiring decisions. Allow your employees to talk freely, let them say what they want, because then you will have a much clearer picture of who your employees are and how they feel about your company. If they post smart, thoughtful posts, that's worth something. If they post smart, thoughtful, negative posts, that's worth something, too, if you're open-minded enough to talk to them about why they feel the way they do. And if you discover that they're vulgar, or rude, or just plain stupid, and you take a closer look and realize that their work isn't as good as it should be, you don't want them to be working for you.

6. I don't have time to keep track of what every Joe or Jane says, and I can't afford/don't want to pay someone else to do it.

Anyone who takes a dismissive attitude toward any customer is heading for disaster. Joe and Jane have the power, and what Joe and Jane say matters. You cannot reserve your care and attention for your best, most profitable, most desirable customers anymore. You have the tools at your disposal to scale that kind of caring across the board, to everyone who even looks your way, and your customers expect you to use them. Your big spenders and casual browsers are all living in the same ecosystem, one where news of how you treat one customer can easily spread to hundreds of other current and even potential ones. That's a big, big deal.

If you are a one-person company and you want to grow your business, you're going to have to make time to track conversations yourself because you simply can't afford not to. Being a part of the conversation is as important as having a website. Doing it yourself is actually ideal. If you establish the tone and voice of your brand to your satisfaction, you'll create a solid foundation for someone else to build upon when you do eventually delegate the task, or share it with someone else. Because eventually, if you do this right, you will need help. There was a time when companies thought they needed only one person in the IT department, and as the company grew, and as the importance of IT's expertise grew, so did the department. You'll start out with one person in the Social Media department, and eventually, when you see the returns on your engagement come in, you'll hire ten.

It will be the greatest department in your company—a group of people spending their time advocating for something they love, caring about the people who love or even hate the brand. I can't think of a better job. If I didn't have my entrepreneurial strand of DNA, I'd be pumped to get paid to be an advocate of the New York Jets every day.

If you're a midsize or large company, or if you can't handle all the responses yourself and need to delegate, you probably don't have to hire someone new. Now is the time to take a hard look at how you allocate your resources. It is highly likely that somewhere you are squandering money. Maybe you've got a lazy stock boy, or managers who knock off early to head out to the golf course every Friday, or a CMO who is still stuck in 1998. You could hire a better, hungrier CMO for less money and use the leftover budget to start your new Social Media department (which will be totally different and separate from your Customer Service department).* Get lean and efficient. Consider firing any employees who aren't bringing 100 percent of their efforts to the job, and replace them with people who will care as much about your company as you do. If you see time being wasted, that's time that can be turned toward interacting with customers and bringing something of real value back to the company. All that time spent trying to coordinate ten people's schedules so they can be in the same room for a meeting? Figure out a way to eliminate the endless back and forth, or better yet, eliminate the meetings. Too many meetings are simply a way to spread

---

* It blends skills from the PR department and marketing, but it should remain its own department.

out the responsibility for making decisions and provide safety in numbers should things go wrong. Make all the people in your company, including yourself, take ownership of their decisions, make it easy for them to use their judgment without having to run for approval every time, and you'll save countless hours that can now be spent tracking Joe and Jane.

7. We're doing fine without it.

That is a losing argument if I ever heard one. If you're of a certain age, you know you once did fine without copy machines, voice mail, computers, and cell phones, too. You'll adjust.

How do you know you're "fine," anyway, if you're not in the trenches, listening to your customers and asking them what they think? Remember, too, that the customer who doesn't say anything can often be a far more dangerous threat than the one who screams and yells. Everything can be fine until all of a sudden it's not. If you rely on numbers to predict the health of your company, you're responding to shifts and events that have already happened. If you rely on comment cards or surveys for feedback, you're still only getting a one-time reply. But if you're engaging with your customer in real time, having a conversation in which you can ask follow-up questions, you can get clarification and details. You can tackle any issue that arises before it develops into something more problematic. Social media is great for putting out fires, but putting out fires all the time is stressful and hard; keep the sparks from flying in the first place.

Any company that gets so complacent it thinks everything is

"fine" deserves to go out of business—it literally means its leaders have stopped caring. A competitive company is always on the offense. Always. Always. Always.

8. We tried it; it doesn't work.

This one makes me want to tear my hair out, it frustrates me so much. It shows a total lack of patience, which makes no sense in a business setting. A lot of business leaders have been willing to give a social media initiative a shot. They posted comments and tweeted like crazy for six months or, worse, six weeks, and they didn't see any results. Web traffic didn't increase enough; sales didn't spike; content didn't go viral. Faced with disappointing results, they patted themselves on the back for trying something new and then slammed the door shut. If they're progressive, they chalked up the failure to getting in too early on an immature platform, but most are convinced the platform is hype, and not worth the effort. They're like people who have never seen a bicycle who try to pedal with their hands, then toss the thing aside, declaring it a waste of time and impractical for transportation.

Social media is a long-term play, which is why the majority of the companies that have tried it have failed to reach their potential. The fault doesn't lie with company managers and leaders, however. It's not anyone's fault, really. The problem is that the system on which most corporate decisions are made is broken. As the Wharton study that we discussed in chapter one made clear, until managers and leaders are rewarded for long-term instead of short-term thinking—or, at least, in addition to short-term thinking—there will be no incentive to be patient. You can't reap the benefits of social media's word of mouth without a ton of patience, as well as commitment and strategy.

9. The legal issues are too thorny.

My industry, liquor and wine, is highly regulated, and I know how many challenges there can be when a company tries to embark on something new. You hired your legal department to protect you; its job is to be conservative and risk averse . . . to keep the company as safe as possible. That's why change has to come from the top. Only the CEO or another leader of the company can sit down with the legal department and say, "This company is embracing social media. Instead of focusing heat-seeking missiles on perceived fatal flaws in this, let's figure out how to take an acceptable risk and make it possible." If you work in the medical, pharmaceutical, or financial sector, you're likely not going to be able to achieve the kind of openness other industries enjoy. But leaders owe it to themselves and to their brand to push the envelope as hard as they can. I have had the privilege to do some consulting in these sectors, and I can tell you that how far that envelope gets pushed always comes down to the DNA of the company. Every legal department has its own DNA, but so does every CEO, and in the end, the company should reflect the DNA of its leader, not its lawyers. Set the ball in motion from the top, and allow the caring philosophy to infiltrate every level of the company. Of course, ethics and legal considerations matter in social media (maybe more than ever, thanks to its inherent transparency). But to allow yourself to be pressured to give up before you even start, without exploring every possibility, is inexcusable, especially when consumers feel so shut out of a lot of these industries. First movers in these sectors will reap some really substantial wins.

10. It takes too long to pay off.

This is a tough one to argue. Although we've seen evidence that there can be short-term payoffs, the benefits to engaging with customers often take a while to materialize. I can't tell brand managers or VPs or CMOs who have numbers to hit that they should sacrifice the numbers for the long-term good of the company. No matter how much managers and leaders may philosophically agree that interacting with their customers is a good thing, without proof that investing in engagement is reliably going to pay off with increased profit and better quarterly returns, most won't get behind it. How can they, when their compensation is directly tied to quarterly results? The long-term benefits of engaging with customers will almost always lose out to the short-term reality, which is that people want to keep their jobs.

It's unlikely a lot of people are going to read this book and say, "You're right. We're dropping all our other media plays and we're just going to care like hell." But the fact is that social media is a marathon—you cannot reach the finish line without patience and determination. That's why diversification is so important. I know there is a place for traditional media in a well-planned marketing budget, but in today's marketing mix, it's overpriced.

Let me repeat: In this environment of heavy content consumption, I believe that most traditional media is overpriced. If you should see any billboards advertising this book, know that I got a reeeeeeeally good deal. Carve out 3 or 5 or 10 percent of what you'd normally apply to traditional media and allocate it toward social media. Find more cash by reducing the enormous waste of time and money often spent on producing postmortems that explain why your campaigns aren't working the way you hoped they would only so you can sink more money into those same old platforms. You'll see that when done right, social media is one of the most effective and least expensive platforms you can use.

A small company might be able to win the war relying on social media alone, but a larger company should think of social media as the Navy SEAL unit of its armed forces. Small, targeted, and hugely effective when deployed, it doesn't go out to win the war on its own, but without it, the troops are at a huge disadvantage.

Say you spend $750,000 on a media buy, focusing on a well-defined, geographically limited target group, and see your sales rise 4 percent. You renew the buy for another $750,000, this time seeing a 2 percent boost. Then you retreat and spend six months on a new campaign before launching it again, to the same target group, to the same tune of $750,000. Every time you want your audience to hear your message, it costs you another serious amount of cash.

Compare that to spending $750,000 to launch a well-thought-out, on-target, strategic social media campaign—blogging, commenting, tweeting great content and inviting interaction everywhere you can. You thank the heck out of every person who says something positive about you. You address every complaint. You answer every question and correct every misunderstanding. You see sales rise by 2 percent. You keep the ball rolling. You never retreat; you just keep fine-tuning your message and adapting to the needs of your customers. You give them what they want. You don't spend any additional money other than the salary of the people in charge of the campaign. Six months later, profits continue to rise as consumer loyalty solidifies. You grow by 13 percent. And still, the only additional cash you spend are the raises you offer your staff and the salaries of the new hires you bring in to strengthen your social media presence.

An ad or a *Today Show* appearance or an NPR interview is a one-shot deal. You ride the wave of attention it brings you for a while, but then you generally have to throw money around to keep interest alive. When done right, social media, though it takes more up-front time to build a database of emails, fans, and Twitter followers, ultimately provides you with a never-ending opportunity to talk to consumers as often as you want, or better yet, as often as they invite you to.

11. Social media works only for startup, lifestyle, or tech brands.

A concrete company does not have the same cachet to work with as an apparel company, I'll grant you that. But you can sell only to your customer base, anyway. The concrete company's mission isn't to get as many people as possible to buy concrete, it's to get as many people who need concrete to buy concrete. And the biggest challenge, the one that offers the most potential for growth, is to reach people who don't yet know they need concrete. So don't limit your conversation to concrete. Building, expansion, remodeling, real estate, parking, wherever concrete gets used—that's where you should be listening and talking.

People are mistaken to think that it's only startups, entrepreneurs, or tech companies that can make social media work for them (many do a piss-poor job—a study showed that 43 percent of the fastest-growing tech brands in the UK who are on Twitter have never replied to a tweet).* Being small is an advantage, because an individual can really shape a brand with his or her own style and personality. But a large company can scale one-on-one to the masses, because it has the resources to train enough people to engage in every conversation.

It's true that some products are sexier than others, but it's also true that if there weren't a need for your product, you wouldn't be in business. I don't give a whole lot of thought to dental floss, but I might if you can make me start caring more about my teeth. And even if I don't give you an opportunity to talk about dental hygiene, chances are good that my dentist is out there talking about it online. Engage with her, and your dental floss may well wind up in my take-home bag the next time I go in for my six-month checkup. (Incidentally, in chapter twelve you

---

* It doesn't matter that the study was done in the UK. Plenty of U.S. brands are guilty of using their Twitter accounts as nothing more than digital corkboards, too. See "Tech Companies Miss the Point of Social Media," Techeye. net, August 5, 2010. http://www.techeye.net/internet/tech-companies-miss-the-point-of-social-media.

can see a real-life example of how Dr. Irena Vaksman, a dentist in San Francisco, uses social media to make a visit to her office something patients might actually look forward to.)

If you're not passionate enough about what your company does to find fuel for conversation every day, for hours on end, with as many people as possible, maybe you're in the wrong business. Go general if you have to. Not everyone can be the Lakers, but anyone can talk basketball. When I started out, I didn't have the name recognition of Robert Parker, or the clout of *Wine Spectator*, so I didn't talk about Gary Vaynerchuk or Wine Library—I talked about Chardonnay. Social media gives you the opportunity to take your business to its fullest potential. Grab it.

The Answer Is Always the Same

I think we're entering a business golden age. It took a long time for people to recognize the value of intellectual capital, whose intangible assets don't show up on a spreadsheet, couldn't be tracked, and couldn't be expressed in dollars. Now it's widely understood that intellectual capital is part of the backbone of every organization, and worth protecting. While the ability to form relationships has always been considered a subset of intellectual capital, social media has catapulted that skill into a wealth-building category. In the future, the companies with tremendous "relationship capital" will be the ones to succeed. Society is creating an ecosystem that rewards good manners, high touch, honesty, and integrity. Ten years from now, every company will have a Chief Culture Officer on staff and, if big enough, a team dedicated to scaling one-on-one relationships. All of the issues discussed above will have been resolved one way or another. The metrics and the standards that might seem experimental or suspicious now will be well established and accepted, just like the ones we've used for so many years to measure traditional marketing platforms.

In the end, no matter what obstacles a company faces in the Thank You Economy, the solution will always be the same. Competitors are bigger? Outcare them. They're cheaper? Outcare them. They've got celebrity status and you don't? Outcare them. Social media gives you the tools to touch your consumer and create an emotion where before there might not have been one. It doesn't matter if you're not small or cool or sexy—people can get pumped up about the craziest stuff. I mean, really, who could have predicted the guy in a trench coat pulverizing iPhones in a blender? (Seriously, if you haven't seen it, check out willitblend .com. It's fantastic!)

There is one thing that the speaker at the 1997 Chamber of Commerce dotcom talk got right: in the end, it is the businesses that have established strong relationships with their customers that will come out on top. It's unfortunate that so many companies had to fall by the wayside while the Thank You Economy took shape, but now that it's here, the playing field is becoming shockingly equal.

PART II

_____

How to Win

CHAPTER FOUR

From the Top:
Instill the Right Culture

I can point to the date when the Thank You Economy's existence became a matter of public record. It was July 22, 2009, a Wednesday. That's the day it was announced that Amazon had bought Zappos for $1.2 billion.

Jeff Bezos is a hell of a smart guy, yet I heard more than one venture capitalist insider mutter that Zappos pulled a coup. There's just no way the online retail company was worth that much money, they said. But Zappos wasn't overpriced, and Bezos knew exactly what he was doing.

It seems to me that anyone who knows Bezos's track record and still criticizes this acquisition is someone for whom numbers tell the entire story. I, on the other hand, don't care what the numbers say, because I know that no company's whole story can be read in the black-and-white columns of a P&L statement. And I think Bezos knows that, too. I think he looked into the future, and the future was Zappos. Here was a company that, according to off-the-record sources, was outselling Amazon on some non-footwear products that Amazon sold for less. There are only two things that will convince consumers to pay more for something when they could pay less. One is convenience, and the other is an outstanding customer experience. A lot of companies can play the convenience card, but very few companies, including Amazon, do customer service like Zappos. By dominating in both categories, they were the only retail threat to Amazon, and they're only going to get bigger and better as their customer relationships deepen and their word of mouth continues to spread. No one outcares like Zappos. This wasn't a buy based on numbers; it was a buy based on culture and trends. That's why Bezos is a visionary. I think he sees that culture is the next playing field, just as he saw that ecommerce was the next playing field. He wouldn't spend almost a billion dollars on anything but the future.

He doesn't explicitly say this in the YouTube video that he made to explain the buy. What he does say is, "I get all weak-kneed when I see a customer-obsessed company, and Zappos certainly is that." He also makes the point that he believes Amazon and Zappos are compatible because they both obsess over customer service (though as Tony Hsieh points out in the letter he wrote to Zappos employees to announce the deal, they do it in different ways). Specifically, what he says is, "When given the choice of obsessing over competitors, or obsessing over customers, we [Amazon] always obsess over customers."

Bezos hasn't asked for my advice, but I'm going to give it anyway. If he or anyone else wants to dominate in the Thank You

Economy, there's one more obsession that has to take root that isn't mentioned in his video. Success in the Thank You Economy hinges on obsessively caring about the customer, yes, but a great caring culture stems from the top of a company and cascades through it like a waterfall. If you want that culture to flow outside of the company to the customer, and then get carried even farther by word of mouth, you have to be sure that your messengers live and breathe it the same way you do. Therefore, the dominant obsession for any leader running a company in the Thank You Economy shouldn't be the competition, nor should it be customer service. It should be your employees.

One-to-One Management

Zappos has an amazing work environment. There's free food in the cafeteria, a library, and a lot of happy employees. I'm willing to bet that most of the companies that are praised for outstanding customer service also fall pretty high on the scale of great places to work. It's got to be awfully hard for employees to give phenomenal customer service when they're not phenomenally satisfied with their jobs. Zappos' perks, however, and those that are offered at other companies, such as casual Fridays or a glass keepsake on one's fifth anniversary, aren't what actually lead to employee satisfaction. I think it's safe to say that Vaynermedia is a great place to work, but we're twenty people crammed into a tiny space, and we don't give out free snacks or even knock off early on summer Fridays. I work my staff to the bone. Still, I know they're happy, because while perks might make employees think harder before deciding to leave, there are only two things that make employees really, really happy and make them want to stay.

The first thing that makes an employee happy is being treated like an adult. That means that until people prove that they can't be trusted, they should be allowed to manage their job as they see fit. The second is feeling that his or her individual needs are being met. This is rare. To achieve this kind of satisfaction among staff would require business leaders to engage at the same one-on-one level with their employees as with their customers. Until now, not many companies have been up to the challenge. It does sound daunting, but it doesn't have to be. It's merely a matter of establishing a truly caring culture at the top, and applying Thank You Economy principles internally as well as externally.

For example, at Vaynermedia, we recently established a new vacation policy: there is none. The policy is, take as much or as little vacation as you want. At first it threw everyone off a little. What would be considered too much vacation? Then my staff figured out that I was serious, and that they would not be judged by how much vacation they took. Some have taken a solid amount; some have taken none. What matters is that they all get to decide for themselves how much time off they need in order to perform their job at the highest level when they are working, which means caring their face off for our clients, for each other, and for the brand. I don't see how I can make that call for them. Some people have kids; others don't. Some people have family that lives nearby; others have to travel long distances to visit loved ones. Some people just need a little more downtime to recharge than others.

I do have some basic rules. I'm passionate about team build-ing, so I don't hire anyone who wants to work from home on a regular basis. We need to be available when our clients are work-ing, so project managers need to be in by 9:00 and the execution team should be in by 10:30 a.m. But within those parameters, I let my staff manage their time themselves. What difference does it make what time they leave, or how much vacation they take, so long as they are there when I, their colleagues, or their clients need them, they are doing their job 110 percent at all times, and they're meeting their objectives?

I care more about my employees than I do about my custom-ers, and I care more about my customers than I do about breath-ing. I am a naturally touchy-feely guy, and at work I've been like a mother hen (one with a huge competitive streak, for sure), constantly checking in on my employees, talking to them, and, when I can, making sure they have the latitude and resources to solve whatever problems they encounter. I've made it a prior-ity to know what's going on professionally, and often personally, with everyone on my staff. The constant dialogue, which helps me confirm that my employees feel they are being allowed to position themselves to succeed, has made it easy for me to see which people aren't pulling their weight or who isn't the right person for the job. Thanks to the communication facilitated by the open, trusting, caring culture of the company, however, it has been extremely rare for me to have to let anyone go.

Unfortunately, the employees of Wine Library have probably benefited more from this kind of attention than those at Vayner-media. I've had to travel much more since launching Vaynerme-dia, and it's been impossible to get as close to each individual employee, to get a true sense of who the people are and what they need. I do my best—I'm probably an All Star player right now. But at Wine Library, I was a Hall of Famer. I want to be the same way at Vaynermedia, and I have every intention of doing so as soon as possible.

So as you can see, even I, who run relatively small companies, can find it difficult to keep up with the kind of one-on-one employee service required by the Thank You Economy. How could it possibly be incorporated into a larger company? Some companies are proving that it's possible. Zappos has done an outstanding job of creating an employee-centered company culture, and there are others who have made some smart moves and experimented successfully with giving their employees free rein, such as Best Buy, with its twittering Twelpforce. Eventually the companies in the best position to dominate will adapt many of these companies' ideas, and then take them even farther. I predict that one day every company will have, along with a CEO, CFO, COO, and CSO, someone with a title like CCO—Chief Culture Officer—whose job will be to keep track of the needs of every single employee at the company. Not keep track of every employee; that would still be HR's job. Keep track of their needs, and meet them to the best of the CCO's ability, not through empty pep talks and token gifts but through individualized goal setting, strategizing for the future, and constant confirmation that the employee is satisfied. I'd love a job like this. If I didn't want to buy the New York Jets, I'd be pestering every Fortune 500 company who would listen to let me create the position of CCO so I could show them what a major difference someone in that role could make to their bottom line. Everyone knows that turnover costs a company a fortune; a CCO's salary could easily pay for itself just from the amount of money saved in lowered recruitment and retraining resources. What companies don't realize is how much extra money they would earn if employees loved them so much, they took it upon themselves to work harder and longer than they would otherwise. With a CCO on staff to help make sure each worker has a reason to feel that way about his or her employer, companies could find themselves manned less by dedicated staff centered around a job, and more by passionate armies devoted to a cause.

But for a mid-to-large company, being an effective CCO would require getting to know a massive number of people on an individual level, wouldn't it? Absolutely. It would be doable if all the other cultural building blocks to a Thank You Economy company had been established.

Cultural Building Blocks

Putting those building blocks in place could occur only once the company's leadership dedicated itself to making it happen, of course. If a leader were so inclined, here's how it could be done:

1. BEGIN WITH YOURSELF. Since culture stems from the top of a company, one would hope that the top exec has a good sense of who he or she is. Strong self-awareness makes a strong culture possible. Remembering who you are and the qualities that have made you successful until now, whether you're a CEO, an executive, or a mid-level manager, is extremely important as you

work toward developing, sustaining, and spreading the company culture. It won't happen if you try to wear anyone's hat but your own. If you're buttoned up and formal, don't try to become hip and casual. If you're a conservative company, be a conservative company; just be a conservative company that puts its employees first, and its customers ahead of everything else. There's a way to do that without installing a foosball table or allowing people to wear flip-flops to the office. I hate it when companies give their offices a face lift and open a lounge or floor where employees can play Nintendo Wii and eat free Twizzlers, as if to announce, "See how young at heart we are? We know what the kids want!" Self-aware leaders don't waste a lot of time or money trying to be something they're not.

In addition, leaders have to commit to the Thank You Economy before they can tell others to do so. Only once it is ingrained in your overall vision and strategy can you successfully spread it through your company or department. The Thank You Economy is based in authenticity, and authenticity has to begin with you.

2. **COMMIT WHOLE HOG.** No one can be expected to turn over a sizable portion of the company's marketing budget to customer service–enhancing social media initiatives overnight, but the mental commitment can be made in a millisecond. The mental commitment is probably even more important than the financial commitment, especially in the early stages of preparing a company for the Thank You Economy. After all, there are going to be speed bumps and wrong turns and flat tires along the way. But if the leaders of the company are unwavering in their

determination to create a culture of supersized caring, none of those setbacks will slow the company down for long. At the same time that you're weaving care-your-face-off cultural DNA into the company, you can closely analyze your spending so you can take a practical approach to finding the money you need to implement creative, authentic social media initiatives. Stop blindly spending, reexamine your staff, start haggling harder for the best deals, and revisit the agencies and vendors you work with. The money is there; it's just being spent in the wrong place.

3. SET THE TONE. As soon as leaders commit to building a caring culture, they need to send a strong, direct message about their intent. Employees should be able to feel the difference immediately, and they should be able to look to their leaders for examples of the kind of care, concern, and one-on-one interaction with customers that will be expected of them.

John Pepper, the CEO of Boloco, a Boston-based burrito chain, has done this brilliantly. Internally, he and his cofounders have made it clear that the welfare and future of Boloco's employees are paramount, from providing health care to all full-time and most hourly employees to offering English and Spanish classes to all staff in an effort to improve in-house communication and allow non–English-speaking workers to rise to roles of greater responsibility. His employees can also look to him as a role model. His engagements on social media offer plenty of examples of the kind of personal, caring interaction he expects them to engage in with customers. For example, by searching Twitter for the word "Boloco," he caught someone sitting right outside a store located on the Boston Commons, complaining that the music was set too loud. He alerted the manager, who immediately lowered the volume and then came out to make sure the music level was set to the customer's satisfaction.

What followed next should prove the impact of the Thank You Economy.

- The happy customer sent out a new tweet praising Boloco for its customer service.
- Many of her followers started twittering about what had just happened.
- She then wrote an entire blog post about her experience, which you can read about in her post, "Music, Burritos, and the Impact of a Tweet," on her blog, *Rachel Levy*: *Social Media and Marketing*.
- The story got retold in a book.
- A lot more people have now heard of Boloco and its awesome burritos.

Would you care to put a dollar amount on the earned media Boloco gained through one great act of customer service? (I hope it's a lot, because that would mean many people had bought this book!)

More dramatically, Pepper sets the tone by sidestepping around the corporate-speak walls most leaders hide behind. You can see it in the way he answers customer comments from the heart. A perfect and praiseworthy example is the letter he wrote to a customer who was disappointed that Boloco had taken his favorite burrito off the menu.

––Original Message––

From: John Pepper [mailto:pepper@boloco.com]
Sent: Tuesday, January 24, 2006 8:31 P.M.
To: Ben
Subject: RE: Boloco.com: customer response

Ben,

First of all, thanks for your note. We always appreciate hearing from customers . . . even if we've done something that doesn't make them happy, it helps us a great deal.

We worried a lot about Roasted Veggies and what the reaction would be. The reason they disappeared in the first place is because so few people actually ordered them, and the amount of prep time and waste (because they'd sit too long and we'd have to throw them out) stopped justifying keeping them on the menu years ago . . . but because of the few, and outspoken, customers who lived on them, we kept them in place. You are now the 7th person that has written about this loss since we took them off three months ago (not including a handful of our employees who are also quite upset).

From a purely business standpoint, it didn't make any sense to keep the Roasted Veggies. From a customer loyalty standpoint, however, your note (and the others like it) makes me want to get them back on the menu tomorrow! The challenge we always have is balancing the two . . . you would be amazed at the number of requests we get on a weekly basis from our customers—obviously, we can't accommodate everyone, but we do listen to everyone, and consider what they say carefully.

I don't know how this will turn out in the months to come. I know I can't promise they will return unless we start hearing overwhelming feedback that they must. We've taken items off in the past and had no choice but to bring them back (ie. Buffalo chicken is best example where it felt like a riot was about to take place) . . . so far, this hasn't been one of those items.

I hate to even suggest trying the tofu, if you are in fact a vegetarian. My wife is, and that's what she gets religiously. It's not your standard tofu, it has spice, flavor, and people love it!

Other vegetarians will get the fajitas, though I agree with you [they] are far different than the Roasted Veggies.

And finally, others will just get any of the items we sell "as is," which is to say without chicken or steak. Most of our menu items start vegetarian, and only when you add chicken or steak do they become otherwise.

I am sorry I don't have the answer you are looking for. To try and make up for this, and to give you a few visits on us to possibly find something else that gets you excited, send me the 16 digit code on the back of your Boloco card (you can pick one up if you don't have one, and send it to me then) and I'll add some Burrito Bucks on there for you to use. It's the least we can do, and maybe you'll find something that works. If not, we will hope that something we do in the future brings you back to our restaurants—we have sincerely appreciated your business and hope we'll find a way to earn it back soon.

Cheers,

John

This letter is:

> PERSONAL   Not a whiff of corporate speak. Pepper mentions his wife, offers other alternatives, and sounds genuinely sorry the customer is unhappy.
> HONEST   He doesn't make any promises he can't keep, and explains the practical and financial reasons why the unpopular decision had to be made.
> ACCOMMODATING   He offers a way for the customer to try some other options on the menu, free of charge.

I read this letter, and the one written by Tony Hsieh to announce the Zappos/Amazon deal to Zappos employees,* and I wonder why so many business leaders have such a hard time being real. Imagine how a customer would feel if he got a letter like this from a CEO, instead of one packed with stiff, formal, empty jargon. Pepper is walking the Thank You Economy walk, and from Boloco's success and loyal customer following, it's clear that his efforts to properly set the tone are flowing downhill, out the front door, and into the streets. Pepper is surely spot-on when he says, "I know people are saying, 'I'm going to go to Boloco because I know they care about my business.'"

4. **INVEST IN EMPLOYEES.** If you're a social media champion at your company, but no one is listening to you yet, take heart; your time is near. Think about all the people on staff at the television studios in the early 1990s who noted the success of MTV's *The*

---

*   A copy of the letter is included in the Sawdust at the end of the book.

Real World and fought to convince their companies that there was a huge opportunity in reality TV. They had to wait until the summer of 2000 to be proven right with the explosive success of *Big Brother* and *Survivor.* I doubt that you, on the other hand, will have to wait eight years to see businesses fully adopt and accept social media into their marketing strategies. The company you're currently working for may take that long, but I would hope that if you're a forward-thinking, ambitious person, you'll have jumped ship long before then and taken your talents someplace where they are appreciated.

If you're a company leader, and you philosophically agree with Thank You Economy principles but your company is still not ready to implement social media strategies, look around. Who keeps asking you when the business is going to have a Facebook page? Who keeps forwarding blog posts and articles about companies successfully using social media to reach their customers? Even if you don't understand the social media trend, those people do. And they not only already know your company, they already care enough to be thinking of ways to help it grow. Even if this whole social media thing were to wind up being a load of nothing (which isn't going to happen), any person willing to put him- or herself on the line like that is one of the most valuable in your company. Do not let such employees get so frustrated by your refusal to listen to new ideas that they decide to leave. Too many leaders invest insufficiently in their employees for fear of losing out when those employees leave. Any investment you make in your employees will be safe if they believe that you really care about them and their future. Create a culture that rewards people who show that they care. Seek the input of people who have shown a tendency to take risks and share big ideas. Prove that you value your employees above all else by giving them the freedom to ask for what they want, to experiment, and to be themselves.

It's okay if you put this effort into employees and they still choose to leave for bigger and better positions at other companies. You want ambitious people on staff, and it's inevitable that ambitious people will be on the lookout for new opportunities. Even if they leave, your efforts will not have been wasted, for you will be developing your company's reputation as a place where people in your field can grow their careers. That's the kind of reputation that attracts the best and the brightest, which is exactly who you want working with you. Besides, if you've really built a company that values its staff, many employees will try to return, bringing with them more experience, stronger skills, and a broader perspective, because they miss their old work environment so much.

When people are happy, they want to make other people happy. Therefore, if success in the Thank You Economy is contingent on making your customers so happy they could cry, you have to do the same for your employees.

5. Trust your people. I'm pretty good at recognizing one of my own, so the employees I hire tend to be people who share a lot of my DNA. That's one of the reasons why I know I can give them so much freedom—most of them are built like me, and share, or at least do their best to keep up with, my over-the-top work ethic. Creating a Thank You Economy culture will become easier and easier as you begin hiring people who share your commitment

to caring. It will be easy to spot the people already on staff who can't adapt or just don't get the concept, and as they leave you will replace them with others who share your DNA. An NBA team doesn't hire people who can't shoot a basketball. An exec wouldn't hire a disorganized administrative assistant.

When you know without a doubt that you've made good hires, it's easy to give employees the freedom they need to give the kind of one-on-one customer service that will resonate in the TYE. Create a culture of openness. Let your employees blog and tweet as much as they like, the way the Twelpforce does at Best Buy. And let them be themselves. Authenticity is a huge part of what makes social media initiatives work. In addition, allowing your employees to use Twitter, YouTube, Quora, Facebook, and blog posts to talk about your brand and their work not only provides them a venue for expression, it gives you, or your CCO, another window through which you can see how they do their job. Combine those observations with the ones you make about their performance on the job, and you'll quickly know who's a superstar and who needs some more training. In addition, you'll know how they feel about their job, and that is no small issue. There's a reason employees become dissatisfied or frustrated—take the time to find out what it is, and work with them to resolve the situation.

Employees have to be held accountable for their actions, of course. If someone tweets out, "I hate this job and my boss is a weasel," well, yeah, that can't be overlooked. But it doesn't necessarily mean that person gets fired. He might; he might not. It would all depend on the conversation that ensued, which does not begin, "What the hell do you think you're doing?" but with a more reasonable, "Tell me why you tweeted that."

Even if you decide it is a fireable offense, your employee should know that you understand why he did what he did. One year, the day before Christmas, I asked one of my top guys how he was doing. He looked me right in the eye and said, "I bleeping hate this place and I hate you." Well, I hadn't seen that coming. Did I appreciate getting cursed out by an employee? Not at all. But I knew him well, which means I knew that there were circumstances in his life that might make his already hot temper flare up. We talked, and together we figured out a way to rearrange his workload so that he didn't feel as if his back was against a wall. He was a stock boy back then, making less than ten dollars a day; today he is one of Wine Library's top executives.

This event happened several years ago. Had it occurred more recently, it's possible that instead of blowing up in my face, privately, this employee might have tweeted out his frustration to the world. Totally unacceptable. But I probably would have handled the situation the exact same way. I believe in second chances, and if I have done my job and gotten to know my employees and what drives them, I should be able to work with them to make sure something like that never happens again.

Too many companies are afraid of openness, but if you're doing everything right internally, and hiring the right people, there shouldn't be anything to fear. We are a capitalist society, but the majority of businesses are taking a communist approach toward allowing their employees to use their voice on social media. They don't want the wrong message to get out, but if they create the right internal culture, it's unlikely there will be a wrong message.

But there's still a risk, right? What if someone does say something he or she shouldn't, something that could negatively affect you or your brand? There's very little an employee can say to hurt your company that you can't fix if you act with speed and good intent. Much of the negative fallout from business disasters can be traced more directly to the boneheaded way a snafu was handled than to the actual mistake, misunderstanding, or even crime. Most consumers are smart enough to know that one rogue employee doesn't represent an entire large company, and a sincere apology from the top, one that acknowledges the harm done and that offers evidence that it won't happen again, goes an exceedingly long way.

Best Buy normally deserves praise for the way it has empowered its staff by allowing employees to tweet, but it still has some work to do. A manager found a popular satirical animated video pitting EVO versus iPhone 4 on YouTube, and realized a store employee had created it. Though the video didn't mention Best Buy, other less popular videos the employee created did, and the company felt that the popular video was criticizing the iPhone. Anxious to prove that they expected their employees to respect all of the brands they carried, they asked the employee to quit. He refused, so they suspended him while figuring out how to handle the situation. In the meantime, the story got out, was reported by the blogosphere, and all of a sudden Best Buy found itself looking stupid and defending itself. In the end they didn't fire the employee, but unsurprisingly, he quit.

Were Best Buy's actions enough to impact their stock price or the balance sheet? Not at all. But they got some negative earned media that didn't make them look very good to their high-tech consumer base, and that's never a good thing. You would be stunned by how many customers and employees have changed their attitude toward the Best Buy brand as a result of the poor way they handled the situation.

6. BE AUTHENTIC. Corporate execs could learn a lot from Jim Joyce, the umpire who blew a perfect game for Detroit Tigers pitcher Armando Galarraga during the 2010 season after incorrectly ruling that Cleveland Indians' Jason Donald was safe on first base. It was a mistake, a big one that must have been a terrible blow to Galarraga. And yet Galarraga himself couldn't hold the mistake against Joyce when he saw how genuinely distraught the umpire was at having robbed the player of a historic game. "I say many times: Nobody's perfect," Galarraga said. "Everybody makes a mistake. I'm sure he don't want to make that call. You see that guy last night, he feels really bad. He don't even change. The other umpires shower, eat. He was sitting in the seat [and saying], 'I'm so sorry.'"

As was to be expected, fans were outraged, some, unfortunately, taking their fury to an ugly extreme by threatening Joyce's family, "but as word spread of Joyce's admission, apology and anguish, he and Galarraga became shining examples of sportsmanship and forgiveness."

By the next day, Detroit fans applauded the umpire crew as they arrived on the field for that day's game against the Indians. Joyce's humility and authenticity, his genuine remorse, and his willingness to speak from the heart—"I took something away from him . . . and if I could, I would give it back in a minute"— quickly turned public opinion around. For that matter, we can all take a cue from the other player in this story, Galarraga, who made a point of shaking the ump's hand as he handed over the lineup card, behaving graciously in a situation when many would have let their disappointment get the better of them.

Only a few weeks after Joyce botched the call, he was voted baseball's best umpire in a poll of one hundred Major League players, published by *ESPN The Magazine Baseball Confidential*. Over his twenty-two years in the majors, he has built such a strong, well-respected, authentic personal brand that even a massive mistake like the one he made with regard to Galarraga could not destroy his career. Legacy trumps everything. Any business, whether in business twenty-two years or twenty-two days, would be well advised to take a page from this umpire's rule book.

People can smell BS even across an oil-slicked Gulf. With the power of social media to spread articles, images, videos, and audio recordings around the world in minutes, authenticity, and the long-term relationships that can result from authentic interaction with consumers, will almost always be the deciding factor in how a brand or company survives a false step in the Thank You Economy.

Empower People

I like to imagine that midsize and large companies will open something that I would love to call the Give A Crap department (I actually have another name for it, but I try to leave the really bad curse words for my onstage talks). For the purposes of this book, I'll call it the Social Media department, headed by a community manager, and populated by a small army of champion carers dedicated to interacting and engaging with every customer they can find. But in the Thank You Economy, big companies behave a lot more like small companies. In small companies, employees often serve multiple roles and it's expected that they will pitch in wherever they are needed. So, like the staff of a small mom-and-pop shop, every big business competing in the Thank You Economy would empower all of their employees to provide phenomenal customer service, and not strictly relegate that task to the Social Media department. Customer service could now look like the business analyst who works in the Vitamin Water accounts payable department; at the park on a Saturday, he sits down on a bench just as a guy takes a swig from a Dragonfruit flavor Vitamin Water and says to his buddy, "I love this flavor." The analyst whips out his card and says, "I'm so glad you like it. Email me and I'll send you an online code for a free case. Thanks for enjoying our beverage!" If the analyst worked for a company that didn't have the resources to offer free product, a simple "I work for Vitamin Water. I'm so glad you like our product. Thanks for drinking it." will still knock an unsuspecting customer's socks off. It's still so rare for anyone to be personally acknowledged by a brand that the impact of such a simple, polite gesture on a customer's buying habits could be huge. When it comes to customer care in the Thank You Economy, there is little difference between online and offline behavior. It's all public. Anytime your brand or product is mentioned or used is an opportunity to say *"Thank you,"* as well as *"You're welcome," "I'm sorry," "How so?" "Is that how you really feel?" "Tell me what happened," "How can I fix the problem?"* or *"Allow me."*

Now wait a minute, you're thinking. There are a couple of obvious reasons why such a strategy would never work.

1. It's nice for customers to feel appreciated and cared for, but how does giving away free stuff pay off?

Well, what if each employee were given his or her own marketing budget, say $200, which could be spent however the employee wished on providing fabulous moments of customer service? You could track who used their budget, and how, and then adjust. Margot is spending her budget on people who become return customers, which means one of two things: she really knows how to make a potential customer feel that she cares about their business, or she's very good at recognizing individuals who really do need your product or service. The money Dan spends, however, seems to be bringing in friends or one-shot purchases. Now you know that you should increase Margot's budget and decrease Dan's. Or, if you want Dan to do a better job, offer an incentive that for every return customer, the employee who thanked the customer and brought in the business will get a percentage of the purchase, or a small bonus.

It could work.

2. Even if it did work, it could result in people staging product placement opportunities just so they could get free services and merchandise. Or, on the flip side, it could result in a horrible backlash against what could be perceived as sneaky marketing tactics.

Maybe. It's possible that if businesses adopted such a strategy we'd all feel as though we couldn't trust anyone's opinions anymore, and that every time a stranger sat down next to us we'd have to worry he or she was eavesdropping. I don't think that will happen, because I think it is an infinitesimal percentage of companies who would actually go to this extreme to prove they're listening to their customers. But if it did happen, it would take a long, long, long time. And by the time the public started getting annoyed, you, who are always looking ahead to new opportunities to show your customers you care, would have adapted and moved on. You would have already seen what was happening and figured out a new way to interact with consumers. You'll do the same thing with Facebook and Twitter. When those platforms stop working as well as they do now, it won't matter to you because you'll already have jumped onto the next social media train car, or some other yet-to-be-invented platform. The platforms you use are incredibly important to successful social marketing, but they will always be a close second to your intent and your message.

Cultures change. Societies change. An affair brought down Gary Hart's 1988 presidential campaign but was not enough to keep Bill Clinton out of the White House in the early nineties, only a few short years later. Clinton had to swear that he didn't inhale, but Barack Obama's frank admission to pot and cocaine use during his college years was practically a non-issue. Of course other factors affected the outcomes of these men's political careers. But there can be no denial that based on the public's response, or lack thereof, to these pieces of news that somewhere along the way our society and our culture experienced a shift. What seems radical or frightening or impossible or over-the-top one year is ho-hum the next. Perhaps the caring business culture I foresee in the Thank You Economy seems extreme. If so, it's only for now. Those of you who think I'm dreaming too big, come back to me in a few years and we'll talk. I'll be polite. I won't say "I told you so." Well, maybe I will.

CHAPTER FIVE

The Perfect Date: Traditional Media Meets Social

I f you live in the New York area, you might have seen ads for *Crush It!* on a billboard located right next to the Meadowlands, where my beloved New York Jets play football, and on a few taxi tops zooming around the city. You might have wondered why I bothered, especially since I have pointed out more than once that in the past, billboard advertising has brought me about 10 percent of the results that I got from tweeting.* Well, I'll tell you why. Even though the viewership and absorption rates in traditional media are way, way down from where they used to be, they still carry some cachet and can offer some results. To many, you're not a legitimate brand unless you have a presence on those platforms. So when I found myself in a position to barter consulting time in exchange for some ad

---

* See *Crush It!*, page 60.

space on top of a taxi for my book, I didn't think twice. As for the billboard, it said, "Ask me how much I paid for this billboard," and listed my email address. In one fell swoop, I got to promote my book, create an opportunity for dialogue, and gauge people's interest in the question. To anyone who followed through, I gave the answer: I spent fifteen hundred bucks on a billboard for which many brands spend ten thousand.

I'm not that much more of a brilliant negotiator than some of the people buying billboards and ads for other brands, but I had two things going for me. First, I had a great relationship with the rep that sold me the billboard space. I've worked with him before. He's a terrific guy, full of hustle, very persistent, and he pays close attention to what I'm up to and contributes lots of ideas to help me. By now, though, I know the billboard game, so I knew what to ask for, and I knew when to back down and when to press on. Because we have such a good relationship, we were able to work together to come up with a mutually acceptable deal. Second, I cared like crazy. Compare the mind-set of an account manager at an ad agency, whose big-brand client gives her $5 million to spend, $300,000 of which is allocated for billboards, with that of a small-business owner who feels as though every dollar she spends on media is coming from her own pocket. The small-business owner is going to fight much harder for the best deal. How much a person cares factors a great deal in how that person does business. That's not to say that account managers and the other people companies hire and trust to manage aspects of their business don't care about their clients. Many do. Many care a lot. But it takes a special person to adopt a sense of ownership and identification with his or her client. If you believe you've got someone like that in your court, hang on to that person with all your might.

The second reason why someone like me, who built his brand almost entirely via social media networks and has compared traditional media to the Pony Express, used traditional media to advertise a book about building brands via social media networks, is this: I wanted to talk to as many people as I could. I can reach a hell of a lot of people by caring them to death online, but I recognize that some people just aren't there yet. Those people matter to me. I want to go where they go. I would advertise in every magazine, from *Fortune* to *People*, if I felt they were charging me the right price for their ad space. I am certain that the right price is not $35,000 for a full page. That's a figure calculated upon circulation numbers, but not upon actual readership. There is no way you can tell me that every person who picks up the magazine is going to see the actual page upon which my ad appears. I believe the pricing should reflect that reality, and I believe that every company that buys advertising should demand fairer pricing.

Until that day comes, however, the majority of companies are simply going to have to get lean and mean; the only way to get rid of love handles is by trimming some fat. If you haven't done it yet, you've got to find a way to reallocate some money in your budget toward social media, because it is utter insanity for any company not to have a Facebook and Twitter presence in 2011. There are some brands that might be able to get away with marketing themselves exclusively on social media, but there is not a single company out there that cannot benefit from adding social media to its marketing strategy. What's more, a brand that plays exclusively on the social media field is doing itself a disservice by not examining the potential of traditional media. When used to their fullest potential, the two platforms can complement each other in amazing ways.

Extend the Conversation

If you were on a date, and there was some serious chemistry, you wouldn't let it end at the restaurant. You'd probably suggest continuing your conversation over drinks or coffee or an ice-cream cone. You might take a walk, duck into a bookstore, or stop in at the retro vinyl shop. If you're on a fabulous date, you don't want the night to end, and you're going to try to find any way you can to keep the conversation and connection going.

Combining traditional and social media can allow you to do the same thing when talking to people about your brand. Denny's, for example, had a great TV date with its customers during the 2010 Super Bowl. It ran three commercials announcing that for a few hours on the following Tuesday, you could come in for a free Grand Slam breakfast. The ads were funny and creative—chickens freaking out over how many eggs they were going to have to lay for the event—but what a missed opportunity to leverage all the people watching the ads with their laptops open in front of them! All Denny's had to do was say, "Go to Facebook.com/Denny's right now, become a fan [an option that was supplanted by the "Like" button], and receive a coupon for an additional free large OJ." Hundreds of thousands—maybe millions—of people would have gone to the site, spent some time engaging with the Denny's brand, and gotten their coupon, and Denny's would have had data that they could use and reuse for years. So, Denny's spent about $10 million to produce three ads and gave away a lot of free product. They gave their customer a nice experience and more than likely gained some new customers, too. But had Denny's established relationships with their customers on a social networking site, they would have stretched the value of those $10 million. By clicking "Like" on a brand's Facebook page, customers show their willingness to offer data about themselves that allows the brand to communicate directly with them and tailor its marketing in an extremely personal, customized way. As the consumer-brand engagement shows up in the consumer's newsfeed, the message spreads even farther through the social media ecosystem with no additional effort by the brand. If Denny's had extended the conversation, the date might have ended with an invitation for a nightcap instead of a chaste kiss at the door.

Reebok, on the other hand, invited its audience in for a drink with its television ad for Speedwick training T-shirts. It featured Stanley Cup champions Sidney Crosby and his Pittsburgh Penguins teammate Maxime Talbot as they paid a visit to Crosby's childhood home in Nova Scotia. The ad shows Crosby and Talbot heading down to the basement, where they admire the dent-riddled clothes dryer that caught every puck Crosby didn't get into his practice net. The two start shooting pucks into the open dryer—first to get nine in wins. Talbot is leading 3–1 when the screen abruptly goes black and the words "See who wins at Facebook.com/reebokhockey" appear. Only by becoming a fan could viewers find out who won.

The ad showed off the brand in an entertaining, even personal way, inviting hockey fans into the inner life of a favorite player. Then it drew them in even further by giving them a reason to follow the brand to Facebook. And follow they did. In a short amount of time, Reebok saw their numbers jump by the tens of thousands. In and of themselves, numbers mean nothing—it's the quality of one's followers and fans that really matters, not the quantity. But in this case, Reebok had both, and the numbers represented tens of thousands of people who gave Reebok permission to remarket to them. In turn, they have the potential to fan Reebok's message out to millions of people through status updates, comments, and other forms of engagement. Three years ago, all of those NHL fans would have seen the ad, and their date with Reebok would have ended in sixty seconds. In 2011, however, Reebok can keep that date going for as long as they can keep the engagement interesting and worthwhile to their fan base. Now that is marketing money well spent.

Learn to Play Ping-Pong

When traditional and social media work well together, as they did for Reebok, it's like a friendly Ping-Pong match. Instead of spiking their traditional media and ending the match, Reebok hit the ball back over to social media. *Ping.* Then they gave social media a chance to return the shot. *Pong.* Anyone can do it. Develop creative work that allows the platforms to rally, to work together to extend your story, continue the conversation, and connect with your audience. Demand more from your ad agency.

It's not enough to simply throw a Twitter or Facebook logo at the bottom of your ad, or show Facebook.com/yourbrand at the end of your TV commercial. That's about as exciting and useful as saying "We have a phone!" or "Found in most stores!"

What you might do instead is post a creative image or text, including your actual address on Facebook and Twitter, that piques the consumer's interest enough to go there to see what else you have to say. Pull the viewers in, and keep the conversation going for as long as you can.

Layering social media on top of traditional media to extend the story is the most practical, executable, and measurable marketing move you can make today. It should therefore be a relatively easy strategy to sell to your team or to your clients.

CHAPTER SIX

I'm on a Horse: How Old Spice Played Ping-Pong, Then Dropped the Ball

Unless you were living under a rock, you probably saw at least one of the Old Spice commercials starring Isaiah Mustafa that began airing the day after the 2010 Super Bowl. With this campaign, Procter & Gamble, Old Spice's parent company, showed the world how a brand can play a kick-ass game of media Ping-Pong.

First, it started with outstanding content, spoofing every stereotype of masculinity they could come up with through clever writing and picture-perfect casting. As soon as a bare-chested Mustafa finished gliding around from one paperback-romance scenario to another, reassuring women that even if their man didn't look like him, they could smell like him if they stopped using lady-scented body wash, millions of people rewound their

DVRs and watched the ad again. And again. Then they started talking about it on Facebook and Twitter and making spoof videos on YouTube.

Thanks to the TV ad, millions of people—women, especially— now felt something for Isaiah Mustafa, and were linking his manly abs to the Old Spice brand. So, five months and a second TV spot later, when P&G marketers used Twitter's promoted trend ad platform to ask Old Spice followers on Twitter and Facebook, as well as users on Reddit and Digg, to submit questions for the Old Spice Man, they replied enthusiastically. People voted for their favorite questions, and the winners received personal replies from the Man himself. Old Spice Man also initiated contact with celebrity influencers, including George Stephanopoulos, Alyssa Milano, Rose McGowan, and Kevin Rose, who, not coincidentally, happen to have large Twitter followings. The Internet went wild as people found out they could talk directly to the man who could ride a horse backward and catch a birthday cake while sawing through a kitchen. Over the course of two days, Mustafa taped about two hundred real-time videos responding to fans' questions.

Play to the Emotional Center, but Not to the Middle

Corporate America and many private businesses like to live in the middle. The middle is safe. The middle is often quantifiable. And you can reach a lot of people in the middle, as you can see in this illustration:

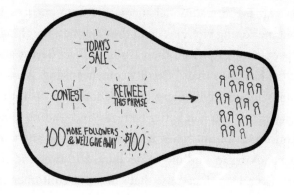

Yet very little in the middle is often memorable, and what is memorable is what sticks. Stories and ideas that catch us off guard, make us pay attention, and show up where we didn't expect them—those are sticky. Sticky stories are the ones that get carried forward, permeating the barrier around the middle and reaching far more people than you'll ever find in that limited space.

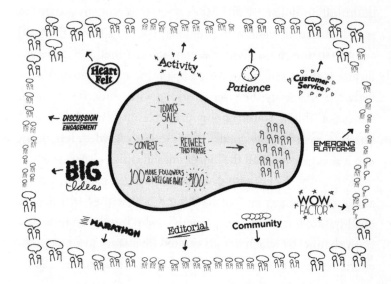

You can use a traditional media platform such as television, but marketing victories lie in the extremes, the things that make people look up from their iPads or BlackBerrys and say, "What the heck was that?" Quality content is king. Always. But from now on, quality content must be followed up with quality engagement. You had better be ready and waiting to engage your consumers online when they start googling and tweeting and facebooking to find out more about the awesome content they just experienced, because that's how our consumer culture works now. Anyone marketing in the Thank You Economy has to stay aware of where the culture is going, and go there.

The Old Spice campaign wasn't cheap. The production values were high for video, the actor cost money, a team had to keep track of all of those mentions of Old Spice zipping around the Internet, the scripts were being written by four writers as fast as the questions came in, and the whole thing started with a multimillion-dollar TV ad buy. And yet, the company decided to spend additional money on promoted tweets, a brand-new and completely unproven Twitter advertising channel. What that indicates is that someone in the company, or at Wieden and Kennedy, the ad agency they were working with, understood one of the major Thank You Economy principles: it is worth casting a line into micro-trend ponds; they are less crowded, less noisy, and less expensive than the bigger ones in which everyone else is fishing. In the TYE, these small ponds will appear with greater and greater frequency. The likelihood is that they will dry up quickly, too. But when used properly, micro trends can provide a fresh channel by which brands can tell their story to a new audience. First-user advantage matters more now than it ever did.

Did the Campaign Work?

It depends on whom you ask. For example, sales of Old Spice Body Wash, which were already on the rise, rose sharply—by 55 percent—over the three months following the first aired TV commercial, then soared by 107 percent (a statistic that included me, because I bought my first stick of Old Spice during that time*) around the time the response videos began showing, but some seem to question whether the uptick might have been due to a two-for-one coupon promotion rather than a well-integrated social media campaign. There are two things we do know to be true, though:

1. The earned media was fierce. Practically every marketing and tech blogger, and almost every media and news outlet in the country, covered the story. The value and reach of that media coverage has to be worth far more than a bunch of full-page print ads in *Maxim* or *Cosmo*.

2. Old Spice's YouTube channel reported more than 11 million views and over 160,000 subscribers. Eleven million impressions—not the worst number I've ever seen. And, Proctor & Gamble now has data on 160,000 people they didn't have before, and they can

---

*   When I saw the ads and heard about the campaign, I respected the hustle it took to put the whole thing together, but it didn't occur to me to run out to buy a stick of Old Spice. Rather, I walked into the pharmacy to buy something else, saw Old Spice on the shelf, remembered how much I'd liked the videos, and decided to give the product a try.

use that data to remarket to those consumers. How much is it going to cost them this time? Zero.

Could a smaller brand with a lesser budget have pulled off the Old Spice campaign? Yes and no. If the talent was there, absolutely. However, we can't underestimate the weight of the millions of dollars the company spent in creating opportunities for the public to form an emotional attachment to the Old Spice Man. But Old Spice could have spent twice what it did, and if the talent hadn't been as strong, nor the writing as smart, the ad would have been forgotten as soon as it had run, assuming it was even noticed at all. A brand that spent only $30,000 and got fewer fans wouldn't necessarily lose if it invested in a relationship with each fan. Follow-through counts for a lot in the Thank You Economy.

Tony the Tiger, are you paying attention? How about you, Ronald McDonald? Why aren't more iconic brands leveraging the opportunity to talk to the people who love them? That said, it's not about the budget, it's about the creativity and the caring. Any brand, big name or no name, can benefit from posting personal videos; it doesn't need to have the production values of Old Spice. Any brand can write fantastic, surprising content. Big brands don't have a monopoly on making social media that sticks.

To recap how Old Spice brilliantly executed one-on-one engagement:

It established brand equity on TV with fantastic content.

Ping.

Then it extended the compelling story to Facebook and Twitter

Pong.

And to Digg, Reddit, and several other smaller ponds

Ping.

Whose users went to the big YouTube pond to see the videos

Pong.

Where they experienced a level of a brand's personal attention and engagement that has rarely, if ever, been seen before

Ping.

And then tweeted and commented like crazy about it

Pong.

Which garnered coverage for the campaign on television, in print, and on radio, making Old Spice, your grandfather's brand of deodorant, national news.

The Huge Miss

The Old Spice campaign is considered a huge social media win, one that hundreds of social media experts have praised, but here's where the story takes a bit of a surprising turn. I was sure that Old Spice planned to use the information it has on its almost 120,000 Twitter followers* to start engaging with each and every one of them on a personal, meaningful level. Every one of those people should have received an email, thanking the followers for watching the videos and offering them a reason to keep checking in. I'd love to be proven wrong, but I don't think that happened.

---

* As of July 2010, the number of Old Spice Twitter followers had increased by 5400 percent since January of the same year.

As of September 2010, almost two months after Old Spice ambushed Twitter, the Old Spice account has tweeted only twenty-three times, and not one of the tweets talks or interacts with an actual person or user of the brand. *Ad Age* published an article that begins "Old Spice Fades Into History . . ." If I were captain of that ship, you can bet that ten thousand tweets would have gone out since July 14, the last day of the response video portion of the campaign. To me, it looks like Old Spice is a sprinter stuck in a traditional marketing mind-set, not a marathon runner living in the Thank You Economy.

So the answer to the question of whether this campaign worked depends on whom you ask. Ninety-nine percent of the market would probably say that it was a social media win—it caused buzz, it resulted in a fantastic amount of earned media,* and ultimately, sales did spike. Ninety-nine percent of market, however, doesn't realize that we're in a Thank You Economy, and it is using old media standards to tally up its victories. So yes, the campaign did win—it won the same way a traditional commercial wins. But it could have won more if Old Spice had seen the initiative through.

Old Spice thought when the campaign was done that they were done. Huge mistake. A social media campaign in the Thank You Economy is never done! The Thank You Economy rewards marathon runners, not sprinters. All P&G needed to do was sprinkle a little bit more pixie dust by humanizing their business

---

* Unfortunately, it's going to be a lot harder for social media campaigns to attract earned media by 2012 or so, once the public has become used to communicating directly with brands. As with almost all attention-grabbing efforts, you have to constantly reinvent and top yourself to make an impact.

and ensuring long-term relationships with their customers, but they gave up. In doing so, they turned what had all the markings of a superb social media campaign into a one-shot tactic.

Old Spice saw a major spike in sales and brand awareness, but there are plenty of brands that have done great marketing, spiked for a while, and then disappeared off the consumer radar. The brand had an opportunity to continue the conversation with all of those people who connected with them, and they squandered it. They left their customers behind, limiting the full impact the campaign could have had on the brand. I'm sure there are more than a few people who were miffed when they could no longer interact with it. Worse, though, are the many, many more who simply forgot about the brand, and about how much fun they had interacting with it. It will cost Old Spice a lot to reengage those people.

I'm in utter shock. On one hand, I am devastated to see this turn of events and want to call Old Spice and beg them to let me help get them back on track; on the other hand, they've given me a great opportunity to show you how a brand can sabotage a great social media campaign.

I was going to buy another stick of Old Spice when I used up my first one, but the wind has been knocked out of my sails. I mean, what their silence on Twitter tells me is that they're through with me. They're glad that I, and thousands of others, spent our money with them, and now they're just going to sit back on their laurels, enjoy the spike in revenue, and move on to a new campaign.

I hope one of Old Spice's competitors is reading this right now. Old Spice had a huge chance to turn 120,000 strangers into acquaintances, and maybe even friends, but as of this writing P&G made it pretty clear their interest in their customers goes only skin deep. Now is the competitor's chance to show people how a brand really cares about its current customers, and the ones it would like to know.

When I started Wine Library TV, I was the only game in town, and I built a pretty loyal following by constantly engaging and conversing. Later, I watched some competitors try spamming or otherwise reaching out to my customers and fans, trying to poach my business. They failed, because I already had my customers' hearts. As my business grew, however, and it became harder to provide the same level of one-on-one engagement my fans were used to, I could see on Twitter that some relationships were starting to form between certain of my customers and my competitors. When I stopped working as hard on my relationships with those people, a new guy was able to come in and steal them from me. It's no different from the married woman who comes home from having a fun night of after-work drinks with a colleague to find her husband so immersed in his video game he can't even break away to ask her about her day. Is it any wonder that she eventually falls for the other guy? As it goes in life, so it goes in business. You have to keep working at every relationship in your life, whether personal or professional.

Maybe I should give Old Spice the benefit of the doubt; it's possible they'll have gotten back in the trenches between now and the time you read this book. I hope so. Even if they do, though, they will have lost out on a ton of potential long-term business, and will have to work much harder to regain the momentum they once had.

CHAPTER SEVEN

Intent: Quality versus Quantity

I n *Crush It!*, I talked a lot about my belief that embracing your DNA, zeroing in on your passion, and living that passion day in and day out were the keys to creating a fulfilling, happy personal and professional life. Since then, I've realized that there's something else that counts. In fact, it may be the single biggest differentiator in this new economy: **good intent**. I strongly believe that if your intentions are good, it shows, and it draws people to you. Good intentions create a pull. Now, you can probably think of many examples of individuals who were able to fake good intentions to get what they wanted. But I think that the Thank You Economy, which has brought us platforms like Facebook and Twitter that emphasize transparency and immediacy, has given consumers better tools to spot and expose a company's or brand's hidden agendas and bad intentions, as well as tools to recognize, and reward, good ones.

If you've ever considered embarking on a social media campaign, or even tried an initiative or two, what was your intent? Was your goal to get someone to click through or click the "Like" button? Or was it to build your online identity and foster a connection between yourself and the consumer? If your answer is the former, you've just hit upon the reason why most campaigns fail to meet their potential.

"What's wrong with getting people to click through?" you might ask. "What's wrong with using social media to drive traffic to my site or store?" Nothing. But if the only reason you're on YouTube, Tumblr, Twitter, or any other vibrant online community, is because you're trying to attract more followers and fans than the other guy so you can market your message to that user base, you're playing the wrong game and you're going to lose. If your view of social media is so tunnel-visioned that all you care about are the number of fans or retweets or views you're garnering, you're missing the whole point. Success in social media, and business in general, in the Thank You Economy will always have to be measured with an eye toward both quality and quantity. You can throw meaningless tactics around to increase your numbers, but even if they work and your online numbers look impressive, you won't have gained anything of true value because you didn't put anything of true value out there. All the numbers prove is that you've made contacts, not connections. A successful social media campaign is one that plays close to the emotional center; the farther away you stand from that center, the farther away your customers are going to stand, as well. Their value will therefore be worth less in the long run than it would have been had you engaged with them in such a way as to make them want to come close. These core principles that factor into the lifetime value of a customer are cornerstones of the Thank You Economy.

Social media works best when you evoke an emotion in the people to whom you're reaching out. It pulls. When you place a traditional ad, whether it's on TV, radio, print, billboard, or banner, you're spending a lot of money to hold on to the microphone and say your piece over and over and over again. You're pushing your way into the consumer's consciousness. Some people try to use social media the same way, by pushing sales pitches and gimmicks. Their efforts might get some brief attention, but the message will fade and it certainly won't have long-term value; it's just not worth thinking about. If you're going to launch a campaign, it has to be one that evokes an emotion—positive or negative—so that people feel compelled to share. Give them something to talk about, unleash the power of word of mouth, and allow them to pull you into their consciousness. Letting the consumers decide for themselves that they really want to know you, versus persuading them that they should, can make a very big difference in the kind of relationship that ensues. It's like when parents decide they've found the perfect girl for their son. He's not going to ask the girl out if they badger him to death, and even if he did, the poor girl probably won't stand a chance because he's only doing it to get his parents off his back. But, if they have a party, and they make sure the girl is there, and they are right about this being a perfect match, those two kids are probably going to find each other. Then they can go out on one of those perfect dates where the conversation never stops. Use social media campaigns to create an opportunity for engagement, not to force it.

Day-to-Day Intent

The same intent that fuels any successful social media campaign also has to be behind the day-to-day engagement a brand pursues via social networking sites. Your intent should be twofold: water as many plants as possible, and put out every fire. When you're tending to online relationships, every engagement should be answered with emotion, from the heart. You may as well get good at it now, because very soon it will be an extremely important part of your marketing mix, and quite possibly the only approach that actually works. That does not mean you have to write a sappy love letter to everyone who praises your brand. Emotion doesn't have to be wordy; it just has to be authentic.

> **garyvee** Gary Vaynerchuk
> @peterpham lol hahahhah
> 13 Sep

> **garyvee** Gary Vaynerchuk
> @winecountryagt soon I hope :)
> 13 Sep

> **garyvee** Gary Vaynerchuk
> @kathdem thnx
> 12 Sep

> **garyvee** Gary Vaynerchuk
> @DanGordon email me
> 12 Sep

> **garyvee** Gary Vaynerchuk
> @winecountryagt 99% of the world hasnt heard of me, not that that is the goal, but I am triple Z list ;)
> 12 Sep

> **garyvee** Gary Vaynerchuk
> @winecountryagt lol I wish :)
> 12 Sep

> **garyvee** Gary Vaynerchuk
> @drewmaniac lol@missdestructo hahahha
> 12 Sep

> **garyvee** Gary Vaynerchuk
> @kathdem none of it really, just playing the game within, u know? executing on the opportunities
> 12 Sep

> **garyvee** Gary Vaynerchuk
> @jamiebrwr never
> 12 Sep

> **garyvee** Gary Vaynerchuk
> @dhbus proceed
> 12 Sep

One company that has been getting their game down is Quirky, Inc., a website for inventors. When they first launched their Twitter stream, they used it to reach out to their community and attract newcomers to their site, but their one-way feed made it look as though all they cared about was pushing their product. How was that going to bring anyone to the emotional center?

Then Quirky started posting content intended to pull people in, not push their message out. They turned every outreach or mention they saw into a conversation, engaging with people who wanted to engage with them. The difference is amazing.

Since changing their approach, Quirky says, "We've had tons of (often amusing) back-and-forths on the Twitter machine on everything from product feedback to favorite *Simpsons* episodes. Now, we're not letting any tweet go un-tweeted back!" For Quirky, a company built on crowdsourcing product ideas, increased product feedback is an important business function. In addition, the increased chatter optimizes their overall data collection process. Customers are going to talk about a business without that business's involvement, but when a business interacts with its customers, the extra discussions that ensue can reveal valuable data. Any company should be able to see how it could benefit from that kind of engagement.

When doing damage control, or putting out fires, you've got to loosen your grip and share the microphone, and listen, then respond appropriately, and then listen again. You have to listen even when you really don't feel like listening anymore. Think about it this way—no issue has ever been resolved when someone left the room in the middle of the conversation.

One thing that's daunting to many about social media is that it requires you to throw away the script. The rules of engagement force you, or the person to whom you have entrusted your brand's voice, to improvise, and be willing to go wherever the consumer leads you. That's a scary proposition for a lot of businesses and brands, and I can understand why. Corporate leaders are obsessed with staying on message, as they should be, and their scripts are carefully crafted to make sure that message is repeated no matter what situation arises. The problem is, of course, that they can't possibly foresee the details of every possible customer interaction, a reality that is becoming increasingly problematic for them as social media increases the frequency with which consumers want to speak directly to brands.

Some companies want to be able to say they have a social media presence, but they're so frightened of the legal issues that could arise with one stray, unfiltered post that they demand that any company Twitter feeds or Facebook updates be vetted. In some organizations, getting legal approval for a tweet can take twelve to thirty-six hours. Are you kidding me? By the time that vetted post finally makes it to the customer, the conversation and the relationship have sailed.

Customers are unpredictable, and forcing a script upon the brand reps they're turning to for help is like handing a firefighter a single bucket of water, instead of a hose connected to a hydrant, as he tries to save a burning building. In fact, a formal, safe script only adds fuel to the fire once customers realize that the responses they're getting have no context for the current situation. The most passionate customer service rep in the world couldn't inject soul into a canned response written two years, or even two months, earlier.

You have to learn to trust the people you hire to do this job (or do a better job of hiring people you can trust). You have to let your reps be themselves. Don't force them to channel your lawyers or your board members or your PR department (or worse, hire your PR department to engage for you). Otherwise, as soon as the conversation goes off script, they'll be lost. And when that happens, you'll lose your customer, too.

Ninety-five percent of the worst social media engagement I've seen was produced by PR companies that were hired to manage a brand's profiles, pages, or blogs. Please, companies, stop hiring PR firms to do your community management. PR is in the push business; they send out press releases and book appearances and work B2B. They're used to talking with editors, writers, and producers, not the public. They have no idea what's going on in the trenches, and they're awkward and shaky when they try to go there. The only reason PR claims they can do it is because they see which way the wind is blowing, and it's not toward them.

They'll say anything to avoid losing your business. The ad agencies do a better job than the PR companies, because they are in the business of thinking about what the consumer wants, but ideally, try to hire people internally for this job. Select the employees who know your business well, and care about it as much as you do, and can demonstrate quick, creative thinking, flexibility, and compassion. Those are the people you want representing your brand to the masses. If you don't feel as though you have the knowledge in-house, hire a company to get the ball rolling and train your staff, then hand the reins off to your team.

You think the guy who holds the record for the longest customer service call at Zappos—five hours!—was working with a script? The script is meant to push the message out. Your intent should be to pull the heartstrings, but not in a manipulative way. Simply talk, and listen. Talk. Listen. By creating the expectation that you'll listen, you create more engagement, which increases virality, and word of mouth, and a sense of connection to your brand. You may not be able to quantify the effects of connection (yet), but I promise you it plays out when consumers are reaching into their pockets. A sense of connection is why people show up at my book signings, and why I feel a bond with my fans even though I may never meet them in person. It's why someone who wasn't thinking about snacks spots a pack of Skittles, remembers the exchange she had with the brand a few days ago, and throws two packs into her cart.

Push tactics aren't all bad; they can be effective when used in moderation. But the intent of push tactics must be to create a pull opportunity, for that's what creates emotional bonds between consumers and brands. And sometimes, if you use some imagination and pull hard enough, you can create something really special.

CHAPTER EIGHT

Shock and Awe

W hat if you're actually doing a good job of caring people's socks off? You've got the rules of engagement down pat, so to speak. You're responding to comments, tweets, and reviews wherever you spot them, and inviting people to share their thoughts and ideas with you. You're seeking opportunities to join or create conversations around topics and niches that are well within the general scope of your product or service, as well as those that may be only tangential to it. You're solving people's problems and thanking them when they acknowledge that you've done something right. You're even thanking them when they tell you that you've done something wrong. You're initiating smart, thoughtful, creative tactics that have good short-term payoff, and this will also pay off in the long run because their intent is to strengthen the emotional connection already in play thanks to all your other efforts. Always you're being yourself, minding your manners, speaking from the heart, and thinking creatively. What more could you possibly do?

A lot.

If you ask phenoms to share the secret to their success, many will often reply that it was paying attention to the little things. The athlete got up early every morning for an extra hour of training; the high-end restaurateur made families feel welcome with early-bird hours and adult-quality kid food served in charming frog-shaped dishes; the car wash owner provided Wi-Fi. What's remarkable about the little things is that the positive impact they have on a person's performance or a customer usually far outweighs the effort or cost it takes to implement them.

In the Thank You Economy, the same can be said for the big things. Most people usually think the big things are initiatives that only big companies can instigate, because it is assumed that to pull them off takes tremendous coordination and budgets. But because, as we've discussed, the successful navigation of the Thank You Economy requires businesses to reconsider their resource allocation, the big things are actually within every company's reach.

What does a big thing look like? 50 Cent knows. YouTube user Pierce Ruane, a fuzzy-lipped, supremely geeky Canadian teenager whose YouTube profile lists him as Pruane2forever but who also goes by the name of Sexman, posted a YouTube video calling the rapper a media whore for promoting Vitamin Water and sex toys. When he added, "What else is he going to do—50 Cent diapers for your little gangsta?", Ruane received almost a million hits. Rather than ignore the kid, or even take offense, 50 Cent flew him to New York City and posted a new YouTube video of the two of them hanging out together, all friendly-like, on a balcony overlooking Manhattan. The video isn't all that exciting, but the fact that it even exists is extraordinary. 50 Cent was smart. He saw how word of mouth was spreading Sexman's message and decided to take control of it by showing that he may be a media whore, but he's a good sport, too. Plus, it's going to be hard for Sexman to diss 50 Cent anymore, now that the public has seen him grinning like a kid on Christmas morning while kickin' it next to the rap superstar.

50 Cent simultaneously nipped a problem in the bud, made a Canadian teenager and his fans smile, and reaped some good earned media. The public often forgets that celebrities are human, too. 50 Cent has gotten some negative press for bad behavior, but with this one move he humanized himself, and probably made a lot of people feel better about thinking he's cool.

But why wait until there's a problem? What if Hershey's, for example, randomly chose a few people it regularly engaged with on Facebook or Twitter, and invited them and their immediate family for an all-expenses-paid visit to Hershey Park? The tickets wouldn't be connected to a contest or any call to action—they would simply be gifts. Maybe that doesn't sound like very good ROI—several thousand dollars in airline tickets, park attractions, food, and hotel expenses, all to make a very small number of customers happy. But that's a very nearsighted view. The long view is in the earned media opportunities, such as when the *Philadelphia Enquirer* gets wind of what Hershey's did because of all the blogging and tweeting the customers do when they share their excitement. It also doesn't take into account what I call the RCV—relationship context value—of the initiative. A few one-time expenses can pay off in a lifetime of loyalty from the people who are touched by the company's generosity. First off, Hershey's has just provided its customers with one heck of a dinner story. Second, many of those customers—certainly the original fans who were online often enough that Hershey regularly engaged with them—are going to tweet and post pictures and stories even as they're walking through the park. Then, once they're home, when a friend says, "I can't wait to take the kids to Disney someday," those customers have every reason in the world to say, "Have you thought about Hershey's? We had the best time!" and then tell their story yet again. Last, as those customers have more children, or grandchildren, it stands to reason that they would want to take those kids to Hershey Park and relive some good memories.

It's hard for some execs to wrap their heads around the idea of spoiling customers like this, because a large number of people who run companies are salespeople at heart, not marketers; if they can't immediately close the deal, see a unit sold or an uptick in profit, or if they don't believe the scale of the initiative is powerful enough to move the needle, it doesn't feel worthwhile. But we don't do shock and awe because we're saints. While the best thing about shock and awe is how great it can make customers feel, not to mention the pleasure we get from spreading some happiness, we do it because there is always a win. It has tremendous value and can create more business because of the additional clicks, opinions, reviews, tweets, and status updates that ensue as a result. The advantages of that kind of data collection should make sense to any business leader.

The money spent on shock and awe can have much more value than a Facebook ad or even an SEO manager's salary. Big companies, with their big marketing and advertising budgets, can do amazing shock and awe, of course. A national electronics retailer can take the $4 million budget that it normally would have spent on an outdoor campaign, radio spot, and TV commercial, and instead use it to contact everyone on Twitter who turns twenty-one on April 21. The tweet might say, "Now that you're of age, you need a grown-up phone. Happy birthday!" and include a coupon for 50 percent off an iPhone 4. That kind of move wouldn't be easy, but it would be worth far more than $4 million worth of earned media.

What's cool is that you can scale shock and awe, and still create a magical, chemical reaction. For example, what if you made a list of the twenty or thirty customers who support your business the most, and sent each of them a handwritten thank you note with a rose, or some other small gift? This would be a low-cost yet high-impact move. Maybe that sounds a little cheesy, but it's working every day for small businesses around the country right now. You could have done something similar in 1999 and gotten a great response from your customers in the form of increased loyalty, and even some word of mouth. But the difference between then and now is the much greater distance that word of mouth can travel via blog post, tweet, picture on Flickr, and status update. The effects of shock and awe go significantly farther now, plain and simple.

Rarely does the media spend weeks following and analyzing amazing television ads or viral marketing campaigns because of how much money was spent on them. It pays attention because there's something about the content of the campaign that is having an impact on people. It's not the money that makes these efforts shocking and awesome, it's the care and creativity involved. Right now, there is a fortune in word of mouth that can be created when a veterinarian sends a handwritten condolence card to clients whose pets have died, along with a book of poetry, hand-drawn sketches of the pet, and notice that a donation in the pet's name has been made to the Humane Society. The same can be said for a hardware store owner or key employee who makes a personalized video for every customer who buys a bottle of Goo Gone, asking if the product worked, and offering additional muck-removing tips. And there could be thousands of dollars of earned media to be gained if a bakery were to send out a birthday cake to everyone on their Facebook Fan page for a whole week straight. Sure, this kind of effort would take a lot of coordination and many hours of back and forth with customers via email to gather home addresses and convenient delivery times. There would be a hefty initial up-front expense on product, too. But can you imagine the amazing earned media and RCV opportunity? These are examples of small, thoughtful gifts that add up to one amazing customer experience that can get talked and written about, and have much more value to a brand than they would have had even five years ago. What's interesting to think about is that as incredible and possibly even impractical as some of these ideas may seem, one day they'll be as ordinary as free shipping is to us today.

No Time Like the Present

If you are heavily into gaming or active on social networking sites, you now might be so flooded with virtual gifts that they're starting to lose some of their impact. But remember three years ago when your friends on Facebook first started sending them? You saw that you had received that little virtual gift box with the bow and you smiled; it meant that someone had thought of you and taken the time to send you something to make you happy. Companies should be trying to re-create that feeling with their customers every day, especially now that discounts and the promise of free shipping are such ho-hum enticements that they barely factor in to most consumers' purchasing decisions.

The reduced impact of the virtual gift, which I think will only get worse in the next five years, brings up a good question: what will happen when people start getting fifty text messages on their birthday from every brand or company they've ever come across? I don't think that will happen, because I believe that only a very small percentage of companies will seriously put shock and awe into play on a regular basis. But let's say I'm wrong, and a lot of companies realize that they can get a heck of a lot more mileage from a single act of shock and awe than from ten bill-boards. Maybe 2 percent of all companies might give it a shot over the next five years. Once they saw the results, another wave of companies might follow through, but it would probably take about ten years before more than half of all the companies in the United States were actually implementing shock and awe. If that does happen, it will be time for the companies who were shock-and-awing their customers all along to readjust. According to MailerMailer's metrics report released in July 2010, people opened their emails 20 percent less in 2009 than they did in 2007, for a total open rate of about 11 percent. Naturally, that reality has led companies to change the way they use email to reach their customers. They have also changed their approach to banner ads, because people aren't clicking them the same way they did when banner ads first appeared on their computer screens around 1994. At that time, banner ads could see a click-through rate as high as 78 percent; today, banner ad CTR is estimated to be about 0.8 percent. Businesses invest in technology and then adjust the way they use it all the time. Why wouldn't you expect to do the same with social media?

A lot of people are having fun registering their opinions by clicking on the "Like/Dislike" buttons they find on many brands' Facebook pages, but their enthusiasm won't last forever. However, just because an initiative that works today won't necessarily work at the same level in the future is no reason to ignore the opportunities it offers you to engage with customers right now. Any data you collect helps paint a picture of your customers' needs, wants, and interests. Though you may need to redirect your efforts when it stops working as well as it does now, your effort to connect with your customers at an emotional level should remain exactly where it's always been—at 110 percent.

PART III

The Thank You
Economy in Action

CHAPTER NINE

Avaya: Going Where the People Go

When most people think "sexy," voice-mail software, desk phones, and routers don't usually come to mind. Functional, effective, and, ideally, completely unnoticed by the outside world, communications systems are the Spanx that support companies so they can perform with confidence and at their best. Avaya, known for developing high-performing, even bulletproof business communications applications, systems, and services, sells some decidedly practical, unsexy products. Yet it is proving that a B2B company can use social media with the same success as a cool lifestyle or retail company.

The Thank You Economy at Work

Avaya's main goal on Twitter has been to keep up with its consumers' technical questions and to head complaints off at the pass. Originally engaging in one thousand interactions—replying to questions, addressing comments, et cetera—per week, the social media team now fields almost four thousand. They also developed a product that can alert the customer service department when disgruntled tweets need to be addressed. The company estimates that by adopting this method, they've avoided losing approximately fifty customers, at an average cost of sale to replace them of about $10,000.

One day, a tweet gave Paul Dunay, Avaya's global managing director of Services and Social Marketing, the chance to prove that paying close attention to the consumer conversation on social networking sites could pay off big. Like all tweets, the one that changed Avaya's game was short and simple: "shoretel or avaya, need a new phone system very soon." Dunay replied almost immediately, "We have some highly trained techs who can help you understand your needs best and help you make an objective decision. Give me a call.'" Thirteen days later, Avaya had made a quarter-million-dollar sale to the tweeter, who then tweeted, ". . . we have selected AVAYA as our new phone system. Excited by the technology and benefits. . . ."*

What Avaya Did Right

IT SHOWED UP. The $250,000 sale might not have happened if Avaya hadn't been on Twitter. Any networking or sales expert

---

* For more details about Avaya's social media efforts and this story, read Casey Hibbard's article, "It Pays to Listen." http://www.socialmediaexaminer .com/it-pays-to-listen-avayas–250k-twitter-sale/

will tell you that if you want to make the connections that will close a deal, the first thing you have to do is show up. Connections are still being made at happy hours and "On the Horizon" breakfasts, but they're increasingly being made online, too. Avaya showed up where few others, if any, in its niche were even looking, and it walked away a winner. Avaya was aware. Avaya cared. Avaya closed the deal in thirteen days.

Too many B2B companies are still avoiding social media because they don't believe their customers are part of the social media demographic. Over 60 percent of Americans use social media (and many more by the time you read this); a sizable portion of those users surely makes B2B decisions. By now, it seems pretty obvious that anyone old enough to use a computer should be considered part of the social media demographic.

IT SHOWED UP FIRST.   The companies that successfully make the move into social media ahead of their competitors not only gain in market share and earned media (for example, Burger King estimates that it earned back over $400,000 in earned media from a less than $50,000 investment in its BK Whopper Sacrifice, a Friend Facebook campaign), they also gain in brand equity. They are recognized for their vision and innovation, for being smart and tech savvy. Such qualities can go a long way toward leading someone looking for B2B opportunities to believe that working with that kind of forward-thinking company is a winning proposition. Avaya's efforts in providing outstanding customer service have been rewarded two years in a row with a J. D. Power Award for Outstanding Customer Service Experience, as well as an induction into the Technology Services Industry Association STAR Awards Hall of Fame. Both honors should carry a lot of weight within Avaya's industry.

IT REMEMBERED THAT BEHIND EVERY B2B TRANSACTION, THERE'S A C. The C in a B2B exchange—usually a purchasing manager, a purchasing agent, or a buyer—wants the same thing as any other consumer when making buying decisions: outstanding products and service, and the reassurance that someone is thinking about how to best meet the person's business needs. When deciding whether to try a new brand, purchasers usually talk to friends and colleagues they trust. Before, they might have made a couple of phone calls or sent out a few emails. They might have floated some questions to a friend while sharing Cracker Jacks during the seventh-inning stretch at a baseball game, or panted them out during a run on the treadmill. Today, though, they can get feedback and advice a lot faster and from a greater number of sources by simply posting their thoughts on Facebook or Twitter. More and more of the individuals who make important B2B decisions, or any consumer decisions, are using those platforms to get the advice and feedback they need. For example, the social media department caught an opportunity to provide some basic support to a frustrated client. The client was so impressed with the service he received that he became a vocal advocate. To thank him, the company decided to send him some Avaya swag. When they contacted him for his mailing address, they discovered he was the CIO of a major investment bank in New York. Every interaction matters. Every relationship has value.

CHAPTER TEN

AJ Bombers: Communicating with the Community

I f you go to the AJ Bombers website, you can see a long list of tweets scrolling down the right side of the page. There's a lot of talk about burgers. The Caesar seems to be particularly popular. People want to know how they can get a burger card. At one time, there was a discussion about who's gone electric shaver over blade. The conversation seems to be endless between AJ Bomber fans, maybe because AJ Bombers, a Milwaukee burger joint started in March 2009 by Joe and Angie Sorge, makes it a priority to keep the conversation going.

Joe, AJ Bombers' front man, has been doing his best to keep people talking from day one. First, he and his wife opened a restaurant that critics lauded for its food and ambience in one of those cursed "revolving door" locations where chefs' dreams of culinary stardom usually come to die. They did it by keeping their prices recession proof—$4.50 for a basic cheeseburger with lettuce and tomato, $7.50 for the Bomber, the same but stacked with a fried, stuffed mushroom. They did it with an awesome peanut delivery system, in which bartenders load up colorful bomber airplanes with peanuts, and then launch them on rails attached to the ceiling where they travel across the restaurant to smack into a target on the wall and dump their cargo into a bin. And they did it by figuring out that the best way to get customers to care passionately about their business is to let the customers help them build it.

The customers have input over almost every aspect of the restaurant brand. They build menu items, determine price structures and hours of operation, suggest promotions, and even guest bartend for charity events. How does Joe Sorge dare give such control of his brand over to his customers? Two reasons. The first is that one-to-one relationships make life more fun. The second is that in a Thank You Economy, it pays off. Big.

Knowing his customer base has always been a priority for Sorge. **The idea that you have to create a welcoming atmosphere in a restaurant is a no-brainer, but at AJ Bombers, online customers get as much attention as anyone sitting at a four-top.**

The last line in that last paragraph is in bold because it's that important. I am convinced that the biggest disconnect for business leaders lies in their understanding of how they should treat customers they meet face-to-face, and how they should treat the ones they meet through their computer, iPad, or phone. There should be no difference. Customers or potential customers can have some powerful emotions when they're considering using your product or service. They're imagining what it might do for them, what they could make with it, how it could make their life or job easier, how it could affect their relationships or family. Those emotions exist whether the consumer is interacting with you face-to-face, or via chat, IM, blog, Twitter, or Facebook, or in a forum.

By the way, tech companies often err in the other direction by forgetting to talk to customers in the "real world." Companies such as Groupon or Microsoft seem like disembodied, untouchable entities, but they have real-life customers and should try to meet them occasionally. They need to look for ways to bring their customers together, for example, by throwing a party to mark an important anniversary, or hosting a video-streamed town hall meeting where customers can come together to discuss issues they'd like to see resolved. They could even pick up the phone every now and then and speak directly to a customer, just to say hello and make sure there's nothing more they could be doing to improve the customer experience.

The companies that understand how to genuinely connect with their customers, online and offline, are the ones that will emerge over the next twenty-four to thirty-six months, putting significant distance between themselves and their competition.

From the beginning, Sorge used social media to reach out and build connections with burger lovers throughout Milwaukee, finding out what they like and what they don't, and asking them how he can better serve their needs. He pays close attention to Yelp reviews,* expressing thanks for the raves, and for every negative one, apologizing and inviting the disgruntled customer to come back to the restaurant, on the house, to try something else.† More than once that offer has been extended multiple times until the customer is truly satisfied with his or her meal. In some cases, the unhappy customers who have taken advantage of Sorge's offer to keep coming back until the restaurant "gets it right" have been converted to regular guests who often let Sorge know ahead of time when they're planning to come in.

Sorge's approach to negative reviews reflects his departure from typical business thinking. In his view, mistakes and snafus aren't something to hide; they're a great opportunity to get more information on how to do better next time, and to connect with people. When one Friday the restaurant's main grill was on the fritz and couldn't be fixed in time for the lunch rush, he set up a live Ustream.com at the front door so that everyone could see what the problem was and what was being done to fix it. He handed out free peanuts and beer. To this day, he meets people who tell him that it was seeing the Ustream video that compelled them to remember AJ Bombers the next time they had a craving for a burger.

That kind of open communication worked well for the Sorges. For the first six months AJ Bombers was in business, the restaurant was at breakeven. In the restaurant world, where 60 percent

---

* If you are in the restaurant business and you are not obsessed with your Yelp strategy, please sell your establishment now while there's still some value in your business.

† It's a perfect, simple play to use your manners, and it rarely fails to impress.

of all new establishments close within the first year, that's not bad. But how to get beyond breakeven?

Eyes on the Tech Horizon

Sorge had always communicated with fans via Twitter, sending out hundreds of tweets per day. He ramped up his efforts to bring all of those fans together to share in the AJ Bombers experience. He started hosting events such as a hugely successful Holiday Tweetup, a day of free beer and food at the restaurant in partnership with other local businesses who offered stuff for free. Then, while looking for additional ways to engage his customers, he noticed something about his Twitter followers. A lot of them were starting to use Foursquare, the geo-social networking platform that lets people earn points and "badges" by checking in at favorite locations and sharing their movements with others.

So:

- He started offering incentives for Foursquare users to visit the restaurant: free peanuts if you checked in, and a free burger to anyone who checked in enough times to become the "mayor" of the joint. That got people in the door on a returning basis.
- He launched a "tips and to-dos" page, where any customer could post messages about what to order, how to get the best deals, and whatever general thoughts they wanted to share. The incentive? A free cookie.
- For what would become the first of many special

events, he also created an opportunity for Foursquare users to earn a highly prized Swarm Badge—granted when more than fifty people check in to the same location—by inviting them to a fund-raiser on a Sunday afternoon. A flash mob of 161 Foursquare users descended upon AJ Bombers, kicked up a great time, posted videos, and tweeted furiously about the event, and more than doubled the restaurant's Sunday sales.

Sorge talked to his customers and built a community, and in May 2010, he saw firsthand how that effort gets repaid in a Thank You Economy. Sobelman's, another standout local burger place, reached out to Sorge and asked if they could partner up to convince the Travel Channel's *Food Wars* to come to Milwaukee and let them duke it out in a Battle of the Burgers. No problem. Sorge rallied the troops and they bombed *Food Wars'* email, Twitter, and Facebook accounts until the Travel Channel agreed to send a crew over to film the episode. Can there be any question of the enormous value of your restaurant being featured on a national television program whose entire audience is foodies?

Only seven months after figuring out that caring enough to invite dialogue, input, and feedback from patrons would encourage them to feel a sense of ownership over the business, AJ Bombers had doubled—doubled!—their revenue.

What AJ Bombers Did Right

They speak their customers' language. If Joe and Angie Sorge had opened their restaurant ten years ago, they still would have succeeded. They've got the instincts and the hustle and the heart, no doubt. But it would have taken years to build the kind of supportive community they have now, and it would have cost untold marketing dollars. They could have had a party, spent a ton of money on invitations and stamps, and they would have gotten twenty people in the door and reached a hundred people, maybe two hundred, from residual word of mouth. Today, they can get over a hundred people in the door and reach thousands who aren't anywhere near the joint, but wish they were. What the story of AJ Bombers' success tells us is that in our word-of-mouth society, if you know your customers well enough, and can speak their language, you can create tremendous opportunities for growth.

They're not afraid to try something new. AJ Bombers ignored traditional marketing like direct mail and newspaper ads—all those staples most local businesses rely upon—in favor of a platform that became available in Milwaukee only in October 2009. At the time of the swarm event, there were only three hundred to four hundred Foursquare users living in the area; AJ Bombers managed to bring a quarter of them through its doors in one day and increased revenue for that day by 110 percent. Any CMO at a consumer branding company would have sworn up and down that there wasn't enough market penetration for Foursquare to mean anything to anyone. Yet in a small environment, which Milwaukee is in comparison to New York or Los Angeles, micro has power. It's time to start looking at early tech adopters as a micro group, maybe even your most valuable consumer, because if you can get them on your side, they'll do a lot of work for you. You put in the heart and the sweat, and they will reward you with untold amounts of earned media in the form of press, talk, and visibility.

AJ Bombers rewards the right people. What's most exciting to me about what they do is how they reward their customers for caring. They could have bought a billboard ad or created a radio campaign or bought TV time and tried to blindly broaden their base. Who would have gotten the money? The ad platform, of course—the billboard company, the radio station, the networks. The way AJ Bombers does business, who gets their money? The customer who takes a chance on them. That's a textbook move in the Thank You Economy. When AJ Bombers throws a party and hands out free burgers and beer, they're spending the money on their guests that they would have forked over to a traditional ad platform. It's a whole new way of thinking about where to spend your marketing budget. It should be pretty easy, actually. I mean, really, whom would you rather spend money on, a go-between or the people your business is supposed to serve? It will make those people far happier than any radio ad, and it will cost you far less. For now, these platforms are not mature enough to command as much of a markup as traditional platforms to get to the consumer. Therein lies the opportunity. Instead of Clear Channel or Lamar or Viacom getting 40 percent of the action, the new emerging platform—Gowalla, Foursquare, or whatever is around the corner—will get 5 percent of the action, maybe 10 percent. These numbers are based on where we are now, but I am sure the margins could become even more attractive when you take into account the ROI of the dedicated team of people you hire to get in the trenches to care for your customers. The day is coming when companies are going to fill warehouses with armies of people who are passionate about their brands, who care about the people interacting with the brands, and who are eager to spend hours telling their story.

Given that, every company can invite their customers to the party. However you do it, whether it's with a real get-together with music and food or a live video on Ustream, you need to show them a memorably great experience so that they say, hey, no one else has ever cared enough to reach out to me this way. You have the choice to spend $3,000 or $5,000 or $10,000 on a weeklong ad campaign that may or may not register with your audience, or to spend the money on an event (one that combines the two goals of interacting with your consumers and showing them a great time) or campaign that not only brings a lot of joy to people, but whose effects spill over as people talk and share and post pictures. When put in those terms, which sounds like the riskier investment?

The Cost of Free

You might wonder how AJ Bombers makes any money when Joe Sorge gives away so much for free. Sorge answers that question in an interview with Forrester Research, "This restaurant in particular has become 'their' restaurant, they ARE the business." AJ Bombers creates constant opportunities for customers to care about it, and people spend money at places they care about. For example, the flood of guest-generated information on the "tips and to-dos" page caused the sales of one of the restaurant's most popular items, "The Barrie Burger," to rise 30 percent. The Barrie Burger was created by a customer named Kate Barrie, and is topped with a bizarre-sounding blend of bacon, cheese, and peanut butter. A peanut butter burger. It's no wonder some people might hesitate to order it. But once they could see for themselves the raves coming straight from the mouths of people who had just stuffed one down their gullet, the comments gave more customers the courage to try it. And like it. And come back for more.

Offering things for free is a well-known tactic used in lots of industries to bring in customers, but Foursquare has allowed AJ Bombers to extend the life of that tactic indefinitely. If you're not a Foursquare kind of person, you might not get why people would covet the title of mayor at establishments they visit often, or check in to earn badges. It doesn't really matter if you get it, though, does it? The fact is, they do. And since anyone can usurp a mayor's spot, it takes commitment to hold on to the position. What could be a simple one-shot move turns into a fun, profitable, sustainable game of one-upmanship, a test of loyalty, and a sign of being in the know.

It might sound crazy, but online gaming, too, is increasingly becoming a part of a lot of online users' identity. When moms are spending real money to buy virtual cows on Farmville, you know games have reached a tipping point. More than 200 million people play free online games on Facebook. Target now sells Facebook credit gift cards, and 7–Eleven did a promotional team-up with Zynga, maker of such games as Farmville and

Mafia Wars. Again, you might not see the point of playing these games, but a lot of consumers do. Go where they go.

Do I think that every restaurant should give away free food every time they see a complaint or negative review on Yelp? No. There will be people who will try to eat all year for free by gaming this social phenomenon. You have to put a cap on that, of course. It can be hard to figure out a complaining person's intent—are the complaints legitimate, or is the complainer playing games?

What you can do, however, is keep good metrics on the client who says something negative about you. If a customer posts on Yelp that he had a terrible experience at a restaurant, the restaurant manager can respond appropriately, tag him with a system like Open Table, which tracks online reservations, and run a report six months later to see whether that customer has returned and how much money he has spent.

Scaling One-to-One

AJ Bombers is a one-store location, but this kind of customer reward strategy is not limited to small, local businesses. Starbucks has scaled this kind of consumer reward to a national level, and McDonald's, Einstein Bagels, and KFC have all gotten into it. The Thank You Economy works when you build a sense of community around your brand, not when you simply sell to it.

CHAPTER ELEVEN

Joie de Vivre Hotels: Caring About the Big and the Little Stuff

The name of Joie de Vivre, California's largest boutique hotel company, says it all. Executive chairman and founder Chip Conley could have named it after himself (Conley Hotels does sound stately), or he could have named it after Eddy Street, the address of his first hotel, near San Francisco's seedy Tenderloin district. He could have given it a name that nodded to the company's California roots. Instead, the name he gave his company is foreign, and kind of hard to pronounce. Yet it's perfect. Bringing "the joy of life" to customers is exactly what Conley's company tries to do every day. You'd think that was par for the course for anyone in the hospitality business. But it's easy to imagine that when customers experience a Joie de Vivre hotel, they realize something has been missing every time they've stayed anyplace else. It is a company that is doing its damndest to perfect the art of customization, something people can experience from the moment they start looking for a place to lay their head for the night.

One-on-One Shock and Awe

When travelers arrive, they're met at the front desk by a host whose profile is posted on a card. It describes a little bit about whoever is working that day, and offers his or her take on what visitors should avoid during their visit so they don't waste any time. It's a great way to start a conversation and set the tone for the visitor's stay, implying, "We love where we live and want you to love it, too."

From then on, it's anyone's guess what pleasant surprises a guest might enjoy. The hotel collects as much information as possible about each visitor when he or she makes a reservation, and the company encourages, even challenges, employees to use that information to take every opportunity to give a guest a memorable experience through an initiative called the Dream-Maker program. Many do it through small kindnesses, such as arranging for a cake when they learn someone is celebrating a birthday, or greeting honeymooners with a bouquet of flowers and a bottle of Champagne. Employees vote for best Dream-Maker of the month, however, and the employees who earn that coveted title are the ones who find ways to deliver an over-the-top experience. For example, Jennifer Kemper, a reservations manager at the Hotel Durant in Berkeley, shared this story about how a mother's love inspired her to create an extra-special welcome basket:

> I met Mrs. Z for the first time in mid-September. She had asked to speak to a manager because she was trying to arrange an extended stay and we had some sold-out dates. She told me that lately she had been staying at different area hotels but the Durant was the only place she felt at home. I noticed her eyes welling up and asked her if she was ok. She then told me why she had needed to stay here so long and so often. Her 20-year-old son was dying of cancer and was still trying to continue as a UC Berkeley student. She had been coming up to help take care of him during his chemotherapy sessions. Being a mother of a son I completely empathized and felt my eyes, too, welling up. I touched her hand and said that I would make sure she was comfortable here.
>
> A few days passed and I had been thinking of her and decided she was the perfect DreamMaker candidate. So I went down to Telegraph Ave. in Berkeley and found this quaint herbal and tea store. I found a ceramic dragonfly mug with a built-in strainer and steeper, and then I bought her a tin of fresh chamomile tea that had beautiful dried flowers in it. As a final touch, I bought her three sunflowers to brighten up her room. I wrote a card that said, "For a loving mother who deserves to relax. Your family is in our thoughts and prayers." She came down the next day and thanked me, and again we both had tears in our eyes. She said she told her whole family about this special gesture, one that touched both her and me. Mrs. Z continued to stay with us until her son graduated from UC Berkeley.

Dream making can be pure fun, too. At the Shorebreak in Huntington Beach, TJ Ransom, a guest services clerk, spoke to a bride whose bachelorette party was going to take place at the hotel. A local, he knew all the restaurants and bar owners in the area. When the party checked in, they were surprised to be sent out on a scavenger hunt that took them to five of the most popular bars in town, where they were received with VIP seating, a round of drinks, and a bachelorette-party game. Upon returning to the hotel, they found their room decorated in the bride's wedding colors, platters of chocolate-covered strawberries, and a cheese plate.

Word of Mouth Works

Can you imagine how many times Mrs. Z and her family talked about Jennifer's thoughtfulness? How many tweets and photographs and videos via Twitter, Facebook, or Tumblr do you think that bachelorette and her friends sent throughout their incredible night, courtesy of TJ? What if one of the bridesmaids had a friend who worked for ABC News, and one of her friends was a journalist looking for a fun segment for *20/20*? How many blog posts about random acts of kindness, or pre-wedding rituals mentioning the hotels likely got written? How many times were the posts shared and circulated throughout these people's online communities? I'd bet my left big toe these stories got a lot of attention, and will be remembered the next time anyone who heard them has to travel to California. What these hotel employees did to bring some joy to their clientele would have been appreciated and meaningful at any time, but the impact of their actions had far, far greater reach and consequence because of the Thank You Economy.

The face-to-face customer care and the personal touch that Joie de Vivre exhibits so brilliantly at their hotels extends to their online presence. Joie de Vivre developed Yvette, the industry's first online matchmaking service, to help travelers choose which of its diverse hotels will provide them with the most satisfying "identity refreshment," as Conley calls it. Each of its thirty-four hotels has a distinct personality, and based on your answers to five easy questions, Yvette can recommend the one that most reflects your own. An urbane traveler might be guided toward the glamorous Galleria Park, while someone with a yen for teapots might love to stay at the B&B-style White Swan Inn. There's something for everyone. Along with a suggested list of hotels, Yvette makes an introduction, photo included, to a few locals who have provided tips on things to do and places to go for travelers seeking a truly off-the-tourist-track experience. Chip Conley happens to be one of them. That's right—the company's founder wants to show you around town. Pretty cool.

Ann Nadeau, Joie de Vivre's corporate director of marketing, has a funny reply to the question of what percentage of their marketing budget is allocated to creating word of mouth: "How can I put HUGE in a percentage? Our marketing budget is so tiny we depend on word of 'mouse.'" Staging incredible customer experiences at the hotels and on their website is one way to get people talking, but the effort to engage with customers is equally impressive behind the scenes.

There is a four-person social media team based in the company's home office that is dedicated to branding efforts. Along with each hotel's general manager, they engage and respond to customers on Yelp, Twitter, Facebook, Foursquare, Yahoo Travel, and other social networking channels. In addition, they are responsible for coordinating with every hotel's dedicated Social Media Champions, of which there are one or two responsible for daily postings on Twitter and Facebook. These Champions also participate in company-wide "social media summits," where they can share best practices and ideas with each other so that each hotel maximizes its one-on-one reach.

To keep tabs on how well its social media efforts are working, the company relies upon daily updates and a scorecard system from Revinate, which monitors and manages online reviews and social media sites exclusively for hotels. It also pays close attention to TripAdvisor consumer reviews and ratings. It should come as no surprise that as of the first quarter of 2010, two-thirds of the Joie de Vivre hotels were listed in TripAdvisor's top ten for their geographical area.

The company offers social media classes to all interested employees through their in-house professional development program called JdV University. Presentations on social media are regularly made at general manager meetings.

Like other companies we examined that are heavily invested in and benefit hugely from social media, Joie de Vivre used it to help weather the recent severe economic downturn, which devastated much of the hospitality industry. In summer 2009, Joie de Vivre started offering exclusive deals on hotel rooms to Twitter followers on Tuesdays, and Facebook fans on Fridays. The first season the Twitter Tuesdays and Facebook Fridays were

Fresno County Public Library
Check Out Receipt

Fig Garden Branch Library

9/18/2019   5:00 PM

Access your account and renew items
Online www.fresnolibrary.org
By phone 444-0412 or 866-290-8681

SYLVA, JEFFERY H.K.

Number of Items: 1

Barcode:59372083331481
Title:The thank you economy /
Due:10/9/2019

MEASURE B AND THE LIBRARY
AT WORK FOR YOU!

More books, more hours, more material

# # #

launched, the company booked over a thousand rooms that otherwise would have remained empty. With very little investment, the program continues to provide a steady stream of revenue that goes straight to the bottom line.

What Joie de Vivre Does Right

THE MESSAGE COMES FROM THE TOP.   Setting the tone and establishing a cultural foundation of empathy and excellence is essential to success in the Thank You Economy. The message that one-on-one engagement and customer service is a top priority has to originate from the very top of the company. Chip Conley gives his employees ample training opportunities, the freedom to think creatively and from the heart, and continually demonstrates and reinforces his commitment to providing a personalized, one-on-one experience with as many guests as possible.

ITS INTENT COMES FROM THE RIGHT PLACE.   The company seems to work extremely hard to balance its business intent— to grow a profitable business—with intent from the heart—to provide travelers with a unique, customized, memorable hotel experience. For example, while any staff member can select any visitor to be a candidate for the DreamMaker program, employees are encouraged to target loyal customers or individuals who might have a lot of word-of-mouth potential.

IT HIRES CULTURALLY COMPATIBLE DNA.   Providing these word-of-mouth–worthy experiences on a regular basis is possible only when a company can tap extremely rich reserves of creativity, care, and empathy. That's why any leaders or managers determined to excel at customer service have to make sure their employees share the same DNA that they do, and believe in the company's mission down to their bones. If they don't, they should be replaced when the opportunity arises. The difference between the performance of a company populated by people who really care and one populated by people who care because they're paid to is the difference between Bruce Springsteen and Milli Vanilli.

It uses "pull tactics." A strategy of caring usually outshines tactics, but when they're used with the right intent, tactics can help a brand achieve greatness. Joie de Vivre uses tactics in a specific and brilliant way. The intent of most tactics, and advertising campaigns as well, is to entertain, inform, or scare the consumer enough that he or she pays attention. Overall, Joie de Vivre's tactics are designed to remind consumers why they should care about the brand and amplify their positive feelings toward it. The individual tactics that are truly deal-oriented benefit people who have already publicly expressed an affinity for the brand. Many are also designed to get people who work for the company at every level to think with their hearts as well as their heads. To work for this company is to be challenged on a daily basis to be the best human being one can be.

Now, I'm a huge fan of Joie de Vivre hotels, but in mid-September 2010, I noticed they were "pushing" a little more than I'd like to see. In fact, for three days straight in early September, they tweeted only four times, and each tweet was about pushing room deals instead of creating dialogue with customers. They're usually so good at connecting emotionally with customers; I hope that in the future we see fewer push tactics and more tweets that pull their guests in so they can experience the Thank You Economy the Joie de Vivre way.

Joie de Vivre has figured out that it's the big and the little stuff that matter most to building a brand's identity. The stuff in the middle is important for a company's survival, of course, but it's the one-on-one initiatives that lie at either extreme—the nit-picky details and the big, grand gestures—that make an impact, and make people talk.

CHAPTER TWELVE

Irena Vaksman, DDS: A Small Practice Cuts Its Teeth on Social Media

There are a lot of people who list going to the dentist as one of the most frightening, unpleasant experiences they can imagine, but I'm betting that few of them are patients of Dr. Irena Vaksman, a dentist with close to a decade of experience who recently opened a private practice in San Francisco. I've never met Dr. Vaksman, and as far as I'm aware no one I know has ever had her poke at his or her molars. But I know that Dr. Vaksman's patients love her, and her staff, and her spa-like office, and the amazing "movie goggles" they can wear to distract them during procedures, because they tell me so—on Yelp and on Facebook.

Some people might still think it's a little jarring to see medical practitioners marketing themselves on social networking sites, but Dr. Vaksman is simply trailblazing where other doctors are eventually going to follow. When over half the adult population of online users are at least occasionally turning to online reviews and commentary to inform their health care decisions, it makes sense that the professionals providing health care should be there, ready to talk to them as well. According to a 2009 Pew Research Center report, 61 percent of adults look online for health information. Of those, 59 percent have done at least one of the following activities:

- Read someone else's commentary or experience about health or medical issues on an online news group, website, or blog
- Consulted rankings or reviews online of doctors or other providers
- Consulted rankings or reviews online of hospitals or other medical facilities
- Signed up to receive updates about health or medical issues
- Listened to a podcast about health or medical issues

Besides her information on Facebook, you can also find Dr. Vaksman on Twitter, YouTube, and LinkedIn. She uses all of these channels to share information, educate the public, and make herself available to her clientele whenever they have a question, comment, or concern.

The Ideal Intent

According to Robert Vaksman, Dr. Vaksman's husband, a lawyer who is also the business's social media manager, his wife opened her practice with one clear goal: to provide the ideal patient experience. That experience would necessarily involve providing the most knowledgeable, current, and technologically up-to-date standards of dental care. It was also contingent on her ability to establish strong one-on-one relationships, possible only by taking enough time during every visit to build rapport, by getting to know her patients well, and by proving that she cared not just about their teeth but about their overall well-being. Yet in order to provide that outstanding care, she first had to get new patients in the door.

Using Social Media to Differentiate

As it so happened, social media, which provides the perfect platform for establishing close business-to-consumer relationships, was also the platform that would help Dr. Vaksman differentiate herself from the thousands of other already well-established dentists in the dense San Francisco urban area (as well as in the high-rise medical building where her practice is located). Besides establishing a presence on Facebook, Twitter, YouTube, and LinkedIn, she became the first dentist in the city to offer a Groupon, and the experiment brought new patients to the five-month-old practice in droves. Unfortunately, the response was a little too good; Robert compares trying to handle the overwhelming flow of patients to drinking out of a hose. The practice was inundated with calls for appointments, and some patients who didn't get the exceptional customer service that Dr. Vaksman intended to provide posted their frustration online. As Robert explained, "The significant volume immediately exposed our weakness on the front desk, which is a very critical point in our relationship with our patients, as we only have one shot at our first impression." Yet what some businesses might have perceived as a negative social media experience, Dr. Vaksman and Robert saw as a fortuitous one; it gave them a way to quickly pinpoint where they needed to make adjustments to their staff and their appointment procedures. Small businesses often have an easier time reacting and adapting than big ones, but more and more it is becoming crucial for big businesses and brands to improve their response times and adapt quickly, too.

Handling Criticism, and Converting It

How a business or brand handles criticism in a public forum is more important than how it handles praise.

Dr. Vaksman seems to understand something that I brought up in the early chapters of this book—the complaining customer who uses social media is a better customer to have than a silent one. You can talk to a customer who bothers to complain. If you think it's warranted, you can apologize. If you wish, you can explain yourself or ask for a second chance. At the very least, you can make it public record that you do not take anyone's dissatisfaction lightly. The platform that gives consumers such tremendous power in the Thank You Economy also gives brands the chance to save customer relationships. You can see the end results of Dr. Vaksman's engagement with dissatisfied patients on Yelp. Twice, people who complained about their experience posted updates announcing that Dr. Vaksman's staff had worked to resolve their issues. The fate of Dr. Vaksman's business rests on her ability to do a stellar job and to earn people's trust. Based on the primarily glowing online reviews, and the evidence that she is successfully converting disappointed customers into happy ones, it looks as though she is doing both.

Often, there are two kinds of consumer reviewers—the ones consumers write when they have a terrific experience and the ones they write when they have a terrible one. Any doctor who isn't supremely confident that he or she is offering the best care available has no business on Facebook or Yelp, or even Citysearch or Angie's List. Any bad service or mediocrity is asking to be exposed on those sites. And though some patrons might agree with reviewers that a restaurant serves lousy food, but return anyway because it's cheap and the one most conveniently located for office happy hours, very, very few patients are going to put themselves in a doctor's hands if the testimonials they read aren't overwhelmingly positive, as they are for Dr. Vaksman. Social media is a perfect environment for medical practitioners smart enough, and good enough, to leverage what its platforms have to offer.

The Power of First to Market

How do I know about Dr. Vaksman, anyway? We live on oppo-
site sides of the country, and I've never needed a dentist (knock
on wood) during any of my trips to the West Coast. The national
awareness her young business has attracted is a result of two important Thank You Economy truths that I frequently talk about:
1) the earned media value of being first to market is priceless,
and 2) the quality of your fans and followers is vastly more important than the quantity.

It Takes Just One Customer

If Irena Vaksman had not established herself on all of those social
media sites, Loïc Le Meur probably would never have mentioned
her unless someone he knew asked him to recommend a dentist.
But Loïc Le Meur is very interested in social media—he is an internationally known entrepreneur, the developer of the social
software app Seesmic, and was ranked by *BusinessWeek* as one of
2008's twenty-five most influential people on the Web. So when Le
Meur found out that his new dentist had a social media presence, he
thought that was worth writing about, and he posted some thoughts
about it on his blog. Like most of Dr. Vaksman's other patients, he
was complimentary and pleased with the thorough care he received
and with the office's use of sophisticated, state-of-the-art technology. He did question, however, whether Dr. Vaksman was using
her social networking sites properly, and whether she even needed
them at all. After all, it's not easy to keep up with multiple Web pres-

ences, and Le Meur wondered how much a dentist could find to talk about. Once again, when faced with criticism, the Vaksmans took the opportunity to open up a dialogue, and wrote in to explain their social media strategy and their plans for the future. The resulting conversation gave readers incredible insight into Dr. Vaksman as an entrepreneur and a medical professional. You can see the whole exchange at Loïc Le Meur's website.

From there, TechCrunch picked up the story, and decided to feature Dr. Vaksman in an article about how small businesses are using social media. In addition, Robert Vaksman was invited to participate in the TechCrunch Social Currency CrunchUp later that month. All of that exposure happened because the Vaksmans weren't afraid to try something new; they didn't draw any lines in the sand.

It should be noted that being an early social media adopter isn't the only reason Dr. Vaksman is getting so much attention. No one would have paid her any mind if the majority of the comments left on her sites weren't incredibly positive. But they are, praising everything from the courtesy of her staff to the thoroughness of her cleanings and exams to her caring manner. Such good reviews probably explain why Facebook users make up approximately 19 percent of Dr. Vaksman's website traffic. The combination of an unbelievable customer experience plus the power of word of mouth has led to what appears to be a very solid beginning for this young business.

Crawling Before You Run Is Okay

Looking over Dr. Vaksman's sites, I'm in agreement with Loïc Le Meur—she could do more: offer more engaging, more creative content and add to the conversations about toothbrushes, toothpaste, cavities, root canals, braces, bad breath, oral cancer, tooth whiteners, and other dental topics that must be being discussed somewhere in the social media space. In his response to Le Meur's post, Robert Vaksman says, "We fully intend to be more vocal on Facebook—and our other venues. Perhaps we should have done so sooner, but we wanted to first focus on building a great-looking, branded and conversion-friendly online presence." I think walking before you run is a great strategy, but I look forward to seeing what happens for the business when the Vaksmans intensify the pace of their social media campaigns.

What Dr. Vaksman Is Doing Right

She launched with good intent. Dr. Vaksman started her business with the express goal of providing the most personal, thorough, and technologically advanced care possible.

Shock and awe. Patients rave about the movie goggles they can wear. They rave about the soothing, spa-like atmosphere of the office. They rave about the twenty-third-floor view out the window. They rave about the tooth-by-tooth consultation they get from the dentist. There seems to be a lot to rave about.

Setting the culture. When the Groupon deluge of new patients revealed that some of the front-desk staff didn't quite get how high her standards of service were, she replaced them.

If You're Small, Play Like You're Big

Dr. Vaksman is showing the marketing world that what works for the big boys like Best Buy can scale down to the little guys, too. Maybe your significant other isn't your business partner and can't devote his or her time to managing your social media so you can focus on what you do best. No matter—hire someone who can. It's not too soon for small businesses to start hiring social media managers (or community managers, as I like to call them). My dad thought I was nuts in 1999 when I insisted that we needed to hire a Web developer; nothing in his experience told him that it would be prudent for a local liquor store to prepare for online commerce. Luckily, I didn't have to pull my last card—the "We-just-went-from-three-to-ten-in-a-year, how-can-you-not-let-me-take-this-chance?" plea—because I was blessed with a father who trusted me and gave me an enormous amount of freedom to do what I thought was right as long as I could explain my reasoning. I think a lot of small businesses are having conversations like that right now. If you're not going to be your own community manager, yes, it will cost you to get one. But you're going to have to do it eventually, so you might as well start figuring out how to budget for it now. If you have ten or more employees, you might be able to save some money if you can figure out whose time would be better spent on social media. Look for the new angles, and find new ways to approach your marketing strategies. Innovate or die.

Even if you're a small medical practice (or small business of any kind) and not living in the midst of a technophile environment like San Francisco, you should establish your social media presence. The customers in your area may be a little slower to get online than they might in other parts of the country, but they are coming. If people in San Francisco are talking to their dentist online, soon people in Kentucky will, too. In fact, they probably are already.

You never know, you know? You never know what platform is going to explode. You never know which customer is going to mean the most to your business. The only way to prepare for all eventualities is to take some chances, and no matter what, treat every customer, online and in person, as though he or she is the most important customer in the world.

CHAPTER THIRTEEN

Hank Heyming: A Brief Example of Well-Executed Culture and Intent

What do you call a lawyer who tweets?

Smart.

Heyming is an attorney who has used social media tools to build his practice within a global law firm, grow his personal brand, and communicate with his clients and the startup community. There might be many blogging, tweeting, skyping, Quora-contributing lawyers practicing on either coast, but in Richmond, Virginia, Heyming stands out as an example of how implementing and acting upon proper culture and intent can reap great rewards in the Thank You Economy.

Taking Advantage of the Culture

Culture has a lot to do with Heyming's success. He is fortunate to work for a company that appears to understand that we are living and working in a world where a culture of trust and transparency propels business forward. In Heyming's words, Troutman Sanders, where he works, is "enlightened," which is not a term most of us are used to hearing in connection with a global law firm. As we've discussed, lawyers are generally risk-averse and conservative when it comes to adopting any technological innovation that increases a company's or brand's exposure to outside commentary. While the new crop of law school graduates may find it totally normal to have their lives, thoughts, and opinions open for scrutiny on Facebook and Twitter, in general lawyers in their mid-forties and up are still leery of social networking sites, and it's reasonable to believe that lawyers in their mid-forties and up are at the helm of a large number of big law firms. It's probably even reasonable for many of them to be nervous about letting their employees speak freely online—even attorneys who know their stuff can make boneheaded mistakes in judgment like anyone else; they have been reprimanded, fined, and even fired for posting information about cases or complaining about clients and judges online. The culture at Troutman Sanders seems to be unusually trusting for a large law firm. According to Heyming, it actively encourages its attorneys to pursue creative and innovative ways to build their practice. I can't say whether the firm has incorporated all of the cultural building blocks we discussed in chapter four, but if Heyming has as much freedom as he seems to have, the firm has got an impressive handle on trusting their employees, which is not a claim many companies in less conservative fields can say. I give them props for that.

Starting with Good Intent

Heyming has created and spread his own culture as well. His passion is guiding and advising startups from conception to money-making maturity. When he moved to Virginia from Southern California, he was frustrated by how small and diffuse the entrepreneurial community was. At first he complained about it; then he decided it was up to him to nurture a solid network of local entrepreneurs and venture capitalists that would help him foster a thriving client base. So during his free time, he started offering pro bono or sharply discounted advice to startups. An entrepreneur himself, he knows how vulnerable young companies are as they try to gain their footing. "Once a company is up and rolling and has a few rounds of financing under its belt, it can typically throw a stick and hit a lawyer/accountant/consultant. But, when they are just starting out and are cranking code in their parent's basement, they barely have money for ramen, much less advisors. This is where I see an opportunity to both build the ecosystem and, ultimately, help myself . . . I am a firm believer in 'doing it right.'" He adds, "Today, this ecosystem is dependent on social media and connectivity. The founders I work with live and breathe Twitter and Skype, so I live and breathe Twitter and Skype. I work when they work—even if that means doing a Skype video conference at 11:30 at night so we can talk to the team member in Hyderabad."

Culture + Intent = Word of Mouth

Heyming insists that it does not take a lot of time to offer fledgling startups his services, and his investment is quickly paid off once the companies get financing and he can start charging them like regular clients. The reward he has earned from his work has far outweighed any risk he might encounter by spending resources on companies that may never fly. In fact, his larger paying clients, many of whom started out as small startups, generate 90 percent of his workload even though they make up only 30 percent of his client base. Some of his clients are venture capital funds, and they, too, recognize that it's in their best interest for Heyming to help grow their entrepreneurial community. Everybody wins: Troutman Sanders, which gives their attorneys free rein to build their practices as they see fit; Heyming, who gets to make money doing what he loves to do in a way that he loves to do it; the startups who just need a break; and the venture capitalists looking for their next investment opportunity.

Of course, there are startups that never go anywhere, but Heyming has no reason to think of the time spent with clients who don't make it big as a bad investment. Entrepreneurs are idea people, and they usually have more than one; they often come back to him with new ventures. At the very least, idea people love to talk to other idea people, which means the word of mouth from entrepreneurs whom he tries to help often brings him new business.

In addition to the word of mouth spread by his current and former clients, paying and nonpaying, Heyming builds business by tweeting and blogging. He says he is contacted almost weekly by founders and investors who are inspired or intrigued by something he wrote.

What One Lawyer Can Do, Anyone Can Do

Overall, the details of Heyming's path to success in the Thank You Economy are not that different from those of any of the other business owners or companies we spoke to for this book. He succeeds because he doesn't draw lines in the sand when faced with the unfamiliar or unproven; he gets that at its core. Work is always about giving—efficiency, entertainment, relief, free time, peace of mind, opportunity, comfort—to other people; he cares deeply about his clients and recognizes that their success is his success. I think when Heyming describes the practice of law by saying "at base our practice is built around relationships," he could be talking about any field or industry, including yours.

The Big Picture

No one is perfect, and I see ways in which each of the companies I've profiled could adjust and improve their social media initiatives. Then again, I'm well aware that there are things I could do to improve my own efforts. Sustaining relationships and leveraging social networks is challenging work. Yet the thing that strikes me about the individuals who are leading the companies and brands profiled in this book is their excitement. They work like animals, and the economy is still wobbly, but when they talk about their work, you get the definite sense that all they see are doors of opportunity flying open every day. It's as though social media has given all its users an equal platform on which they can build not just their careers, but their dreams.

Conclusion

I t's not your imagination; marketing really has gotten harder. Markets are splintering, eyeballs are shifting, attention spans are waning, and the amount of information people are trying to absorb continues to multiply.* Where we consume media, and where and how we interact in person and online has changed at an astounding rate, and it is continuing to morph and expand every day. The only way brands and businesses are going to be able to adapt to and overcome these challenges is by conducting a virtual door-to-door campaign to win over their customers' hearts and minds. That's a lot harder and more time-consuming than bombarding the market with a one-size-fits-all message. Yet those companies that are willing to get in the social media trenches with their customers will see that word of mouth can allow each individual engagement to have an impact hundreds of times greater than itself. If marketers commit to Thank

---

* Just how much information are we trying to absorb? At the 2010 Techonomy conference in Lake Tahoe, California, Google CEO Eric Schmidt stated that every two days people create as much information as they did from the dawn of civilization to 2003, about five exabytes of data.

You Economy principles wholeheartedly, reallocate their marketing resources properly, and find ways not only to take advantage of the best that social media and traditional media have to offer but also to actually play them off each other, they will see an incredible return on any investment they make.

Anyone waiting for the marketing landscape to stabilize before incorporating social media into his or her business strategy is living in a fantasy world. We're riding a really, really fast train; the changes we've seen mark only the beginning of the transformations yet to come. Stable isn't going to happen any time soon.

So what to do? As always, it's about hustle. Unfortunately, marketing has gotten harder at a time when many marketers have gotten softer. We've gotten used to running short sprints, not marathons, and we're not built for the endurance game. That's as true for many corporate-level marketers as it is for many entrepreneurs. Our great-grandparents were built for it. Whether they ran their own businesses or put in thirty years of service to a big company or factory, they were used to working their tails off with few of the technological innovations we can't imagine working without. They'd never heard of work-life balance, and they knew better than to expect instant gratification. We crave both, but I think these will be luxuries in the Thank You Economy. The stars in this business era will be those who are consumed with their work (and happy about it) and have the patience to pursue one small victory at a time. This new economy offers tremendous opportunities to develop huge markets, strengthen brands, or build lasting businesses, provided you work for them with the intensity of Rocky Balboa training for his Cold War showdown in the snow-covered Soviet countryside. You're in trouble only if you find that pill too hard to swallow.

The Thank You Economy has radically altered our customers' expectations, and businesses are going to have to get creative and personal in order to meet them. As we do, consumer expectations will change, and the marketing initiatives we put out that might now be met with "Wow!" will eventually be met with "Meh." The key, then, is to start thinking ahead. All businesses must innovate to survive. Social media gives us the opportunity to figure out what people want before they even know they want it. Using social media to talk to customers is like getting access to the most honest focus group that's ever sat around a conference table and not paying a dime for their input. We have to listen, participate in the conversation, ask questions, and solicit feedback. We have to be more involved, and more attentive, and more interested, than we have ever been. We have to be better.

Part of being better will entail making sure that you're weaving strong strands of Thank You Economy DNA, along with your own, into your brand or company. Then it's about focusing your sights on aspects of your marketing strategy that until now might have been treated as secondary concerns.

The lifetime value of a customer, for instance, is going to become a bigger consideration. The Internet has given customers an incredible number of places to spend their money, as well as new tools they can use to spread your message farther and wider. Social media allows you to get to know your customers well enough to gather a true idea of what their long-term value to your brand might be. Developing a powerful emotional connection could be all it takes to convince them to consolidate their spending with you. Plus, now that purchasing decisions are directly affected by consumers' relationships to the people they communicate with on their social networking sites, staying aware of who your consumers know and who they talk to regularly will become increasingly important. Every interaction you engage in with them will have the potential to spread through their network via word of mouth. When businesses realize that they need to focus on investing in customers, not platforms, they will see amazing returns on that investment.

Earned media, too, will become increasingly relevant. Just as there was a golden age of radio, a golden age of television, and one for movies, social media platforms have brought us into the golden age of earned media. Consumers are tired of being sold to. An op-ed article, blog post, or positive consumer review—the kind of free press that is often an organic result of a well-executed, engaging marketing campaign that allows traditional and social media platforms to work together—will go a long way toward making the marketing initiative you actually pay for stick longer and travel farther in the public's consciousness. It's bound to get harder to get earned media—now that plans like Facebook campaigns are gaining in popularity, the mainstream press won't always fall all over itself to write about them—but while it lasts, it will be powerful, powerful stuff. Of course, the best of the best will always grab the press's heartstrings, especially as technology continues to move forward to allow outstanding mobile and augmented reality campaigns.

Brands should also do everything they can to gain first-mover advantage. Marketers have to keep their finger on the pulse of the culture and keep an eye on the incoming trains. Smart marketers shouldn't ever get too comfortable in their seats. Brands and businesses that can see the potential of emerging platforms will always have an edge over their competition. The brands that show up first on these platforms—the ones launched by people like former Facebook or Google employees—and take the first crack at building relationships with the early adopters they find there will see their foresightedness pay off.

Unless Wall Street undergoes a miraculous transformation and starts rewarding companies for their long-term strategies instead of almost exclusively for their short-term results, putting energy into hard-to-measure marathon plays such as lifetime customer value, earned media, and emerging markets will feel like a struggle, and even a risky proposition, to a lot of companies. The irony is that when executed properly, these marathons can reap dividends in a relatively short amount of time.

The companies that soar in 2011 and beyond are those that will figure out a way to balance the short-term demands of Wall Street or investors with the long-term demands of the Thank You Economy. Their leaders will begin by weaving strong strands of their DNA, laced with good intent, into the top layer of their companies, and allow it to infiltrate every layer of their business. They will accept that the customers have most of the power and be glad to give it to them. They will hire individuals and create new departments dedicated to building long-term relationships with customers and potential customers. They will stop relying solely upon straight, traditional marketing channels to spread their message, and instead allow their content to be passed back and forth (and sometimes around and across and through) as many platforms as they can reach. They will treat their business as an extension of themselves, and care, care, care.

People much smarter than I am have stated that we are living through a third industrial revolution.* But anyone who has been paying attention will realize that I've been saying the same thing (in my own style), for half a decade. The Thank You Economy is now, it's here, it's relevant, and I believe its scale may be bigger than any of us can even fathom. And it's still very early.

This is such an incredibly exciting time to be in business. I know I'm right about the Thank You Economy—once you've tasted Champagne, you know it the minute you taste it again. It may take a little longer than I anticipate for the total cultural transformation to take hold, but ten years from now, I'm going to be on the right side of history. I implore you to be there with me. We will one day dust off the bones of companies that fossilized because they didn't think it could "scale," or because they didn't think it was worth the effort, or because they could not stop drawing lines in the sand. The day you recognize that the Thank You Economy exists, and you begin to take the steps necessary to execute properly within it, will be the day you ensure your business or brand a place in the future.

---

* See Rick Kash and David Calhoun's *How Companies Win*, Harper-Business, 2010, pp. 40–41.

PART IV

Sawdust

More Thoughts On . . .

Starting Conversations

If you're a big brand like Coke or SunChips, your brand is being talked about and you need to address the topic head-on. When you've got that conversation covered, you can spread out to talk more generally about beverages, refreshment, summer, et cetera. But if you're Sally's Orange Soda, no one is talking about you, so you need to do the reverse—create a general soda conversation first. You need to jump into every relevant conversation you spot, much like I did when I talked to people about Chardonnay and Shiraz in the early days, long before I responded to @garyvee's. Once those conversations are up and running, you can start to talk specifically about Sally's Orange Soda.

The Difference between the Power of Word of Mouth and Advertising

In mid-2010, National Public Radio officially changed its name to NPR to reflect its presence online and on digital devices. In an article for *The Nieman Journalism Lab* about how NPR is measuring the value of their Twitter followers and people who "like" it on Facebook, Justin Ellis writes, "It . . . makes sense that NPR wants to monitor its emerging platforms as they try to transform into a digital media company. Facebook and Twitter combined now account for 7–8 percent of traffic to NPR.org, an amount that has doubled in the last year." More and more people are finding their way to the NPR website through links they see on Twitter and Facebook because of the social context that surrounds those links, a context created when consumers opt to receive NPR updates through their newsfeeds, or when they see the content because it was posted by a friend. You'll pay attention to or interpret a comment about an NPR story from your mother or a coworker whom you respect far differently than you would if you found the article through a Google search. That social context and connection gives the content weight and importance that it wouldn't otherwise have. The difference between how people respond to search engine results or a banner ad versus how they respond to Twitter or Facebook feeds parallels the difference between how people respond to advertising and how they respond to word of mouth. One is a random, faceless encounter that is easily forgotten; the other is a meaningful exchange worth passing along and sharing with others.

How Fear Blocks Innovation

It's becoming more unusual for a big consumer brand to really innovate and create a great product. Vitamin Water didn't come from Coke; Pom didn't come from Pepsi. Too many big companies get stuck in the muck of their own fear and short-term concerns, which prohibits them from taking risks and following through on great, creative thinking. They're too wrapped up in meetings and procedure and stock value, or worst of all, the politics of keeping their jobs, whereas smaller, scrappier companies are often still ruled by passion and have the freedom to experiment.

Agendas

There are a lot of people with a vested interest in making sure that brands don't start using social media. You can point out plenty of weaknesses in social media metrics, but you can find just as many in traditional media. The reality is, however, that brands will eventually be able to track every consumer online—there is no truer metric. What would happen if brands started demanding the same metric standard from traditional media? What if they realize that they can spend their money more efficiently and effectively online than on television? There is a lot of marketing and advertising money—not to mention thank-you-for-doing-business-with-us gifts like baseball-game tickets, shows, fancy dinners, trips to Cancún, and cases of Dom P—at stake, and a lot of people will denigrate social media's influence for as long as they can so they can keep their hands on it. In addition, those gifts are often exchanged between people who genuinely like doing business together. This means that even if another agency were willing to give them a better deal, they'd still spend their money with the agency that has treated them preferentially over the years. To say that business isn't personal is ridiculous. P.S., you can start to create some of these relationships on Twitter, Tumblr, and Facebook. Who said social media isn't B2B?

Changing Strategies

I usually see parallels between marketing and interpersonal relationships, but lately I can't shake the thought that there are also parallels between how we market and advertise and how we wage war. The world wars were fought with blanket fire—big planes dropping many bombs from the sky, battleships, tanks. Everything was big and meant to overwhelm the enemy. Then we got into Vietnam, and we couldn't use the same tactics—we had to fight one-on-one. More recently, in Iraq and Afghanistan, troops went from village to village, tribe to tribe, trying to stabilize dangerous regions all while winning the trust and the hearts and minds of the populace. I'm not passing any judgment on how we fought these wars, nor do I believe that the decisions we make in the marketing world can compare to the decisions the leaders of our armed forces must make every day or to the sacrifices made by our troops. I do think, however, that just as our strategies on the battlefield had to change, so have our strategies in the business world. There was a time in business when we had to fight big, and so it was necessary to rely on a big platform like television. TV was a tank; radio was a fleet of planes. Now that we are trying to go local, it's been a real struggle for some companies; big isn't going to help them win. Carpet-bombing Afghanistan wasn't going to get us anywhere, nor will spending $44 million exclusively on a TV campaign, some billboards, and radio spots.

Defending Social Media Throughout My Career

I was the baby-faced kid at the conference table surrounded by wine experts and old-timers who thought my video blogs were a joke, even an embarrassment to the industry. Even when it became clear that my methods were yielding profitable results for Wine Library, my family liquor business, and I started getting media attention as I proved my entrepreneurial chops, I faced constant skepticism and condescension. I got used to it a long time ago, and I actually enjoy the debate. I'm not scared to defend and debate the value of this emerging shift in the Web, because "I told you so" may be one of the most delicious flavors in the world. Now, if I'm wrong, I'll deserve the "told you so," but I won't be sorry that I said my piece. Too many people are scared to share their visions and thoughts in public or even in boardrooms. Having a strong vision is important for your personal brand. Don't be afraid to say what you think. Ever. That said, don't forget to listen, either.

Drawing Lines in the Sand

I think it's sad when someone who says he or she wants a fruitful career refuses to try something new because the numbers don't seem promising. I understand that people crave security, but I don't understand the complete lack of curiosity I sometimes see. Every time you draw a line in the sand, you're robbing yourself of a learning experience that could serve you well in the long run. Lines in the sand will only box you in.

The ROI of Emotions

The ROI of a social media user is deeply tied to that user's sense of community and the emotional attachment he or she associates with a product. You could offer me a Jets T-shirt for eighty bucks and a Cowboys T-shirt for a dollar, and I would still never buy the Cowboys shirt. My emotional attachment to the Jets is that strong. A teenager who loves Vitamin Water enough to follow the brand on Facebook isn't going to be satisfied with a gift card from Snapple if Vitamin Water treats her better whenever she interacts with them online. She may be appreciative and grateful for the gift, but the second she has her own money she's going to spend it on the brand that means something to her. The heart wants what the heart wants. Snapple might get the initial purchase, but Vitamin Water has the relationship, which will translate into far greater revenue in the long run. Those who are willing to look (and there are too many marketers who are not) are witnessing the humanization of business; it will have one of the greatest impacts on commerce we've ever seen.

How Nielsen Ratings Work

Let's review how the ratings system works. Selecting for demographics that best represent the country as a whole, a computer program randomly targets households with television sets and asks the inhabitants to monitor their television-watching habits. Only about 50 percent of households agree to participate, so the ratings companies then have to try to replace the uncooperative homes with homes that best match the same demographic makeup. In 2009, there were about 114,900,000 households with televisions. Of those households, only about 25,000 homes were monitored. That means 99.9 percent of American households were completely ignored.* This is not necessarily news to the marketing, advertising, and media-buying community.

The sample does get broader during the sweeps months of November, February, May, and July, when Nielsen asks about two million people to submit diaries. Paper diaries. Sent through the mail. You don't have to be a psychologist to think of any number of reasons why these diaries might not accurately reflect a person's TV-watching habits. On top of that, only about 50 percent of the diaries can be used, because so many are never returned or are filled out improperly. A quick search on the Internet will hit many articles written by Nielsen participants revealing, albeit sheepishly, that they thought about fudging their reports and altering their TV-watching habits (and some of them actually did). Those confessions are just from the raters who bother to share their experience; how many others could be out there?

Nielsen admits there are weaknesses in its process. In 2009, the company released a report that stated its ratings might have been inaccurate by as much as 8 percent. The reason? Participants weren't using their People Meters correctly. Ultimately, no matter what corrections and adjustments it makes, Nielsen still

---

* I respect the math that goes into figuring out how these small samples can stand in for large groups of people, but still, you can't help but question it, can you?

has to rely on the accuracy and honesty of the individuals in the mere 25,000 homes it is monitoring. Someone has to push the button identifying herself as the viewer; someone has to remember to mention that she spent ten minutes during a half-hour program chatting with the Girl Scout who came to the door.

In addition, as we all know, television-watching habits have changed drastically in the past few years. Nielsen issued a 2010 report stating that 59 percent of people watch television and surf the Internet simultaneously, 35 percent more than the number of people who did so in 2009. Thirty-five percent more in twelve months! Nielsen assures us that it has systems in place to account for the swell in cable and digital channels, DVRs, and the fact that people are watching TV on their iPhones and playing around with all kinds of multimedia while the television plays in the background. I would love to know what kind of technology could make tracking so many platforms possible, but that information is proprietary and confidential to Nielsen, and I can understand why. Still, if this is how social media was tracked and I tried to sell it to a room full of executives in 2011, don't you think they might point out some big holes in the system?

It's important to remember that The Nielsen Company was not always the only game in town. In the 1940s and '50s, Nielsen competed against five other ratings companies: Videodex, Inc., Trendex, Inc., the American Research Bureau, C. E. Hooper, Inc., and The Pulse, Inc. The Claude E. Hooper company was the market researcher during the radio golden age and became enough of a presence in TV, until Nielsen acquired it in 1950, that it was common for television series producers to ask each other, "How's your Hooper?" But Hooper sold, the other guys disappeared, and advertisers, ad agencies, and media buying companies put their faith in Nielsen.

What Touches People

People laugh at me because I get so pumped about the New York Jets. Well, how is that any sillier than standing in line for nine hours to get the first copy of the newest book in the Twilight series? Or six hours for the new video game, Sneakers Smart Phone? Now that brands are touchable, there's no reason to think that with some creativity, they can't create the same emotions as a sports team or a pop culture event. The brand that touches and creates the most emotion wins.

Campbell's knows this to be true. In a complete revamping of their marketing strategy, they are investing heavily in biometric tools—measuring skin moisture, heart rate, breath, and posture, for example—to help measure the subconscious, emotional reactions consumers have to their products. This research resulted in big changes to the look of their condensed soup cans, which they hope will evoke more emotional reactions from shoppers.

The Broken Corporate Game

The CEO of BP left with a multimillion-dollar bonus. He's in charge during the worst environmental disaster of all time, and he leaves with money spilling out of his pockets. When a leader's worst-case scenario doesn't look that bad, there's no reason that person should care desperately about the fate of his or her company. If that CEO's contract had said that the stock price needed to be at a certain level or he would lose everything, he would have treated the whole oil-well situation differently. When the worst-case scenario is pretty, you're never as scared or antsy as you should be. Period!

Playboy Corporate America

Corporate America is rewarded for hookups and one-night stands, and that's how much respect most corporations show toward their customers. Don't hate the player; hate the game.

Billboards

There is no chance in heck that as many people as the companies tell you are viewing billboards are viewing billboards. People are so distracted with their mobile devices they're barely looking at the roads, much less looking at billboards. Oprah is right about this one—cars should be no-phone zones. I'm scared to share the road with other drivers!

I Like TV

Just to make it really, really clear: I am a fan of traditional media; I just have issues with the creative work and the pricing. I see what people are putting out there in print, on radio, and on TV, and I don't believe they are pushing the creative envelope enough. And, because of the massive changes in viewership, I don't think I should have to pay for this media as if it were still

1994 and radio, TV, and print were the only mediums getting people's attention.

Surveys and Customer Cards

When you ask a consumer to fill out a survey or comment card, you've already influenced the answer you're going to get. As soon as people are asked for their opinion, they filter their replies. Maybe they're afraid of getting someone fired. Maybe they want to sound smart. Maybe they don't want to hurt the feelings of the person asking the question. Maybe they are mean. But on social media, you're seeing people's unfiltered conversations, reactions, and opinions. That's a gold mine of information for the brand brave enough to look for it.

"Most Brands Still Irrelevant on Twitter"

While I was writing this book, *Ad Age* published an article called "Most Brands Still Irrelevant on Twitter: Marketers Are Certainly Tweeting, but Users Are Barely Listening." Maybe someone at your company sent this around saying, "See, I was right to insist that we not waste our time on Twitter." I'd like to point a few things out about this article:

1.   The article actually explains the problem: "While marketers such as Dell, Comcast, Ford and Starbucks have been, at times, clever participants on Twitter, the majority of marketers use it as a mini press release service. Only 12% of messages from marketers are di-

rected at individual Twitter users, meaning marketers still see it as a broadcast medium rather than a
conversational one." So you see, it's not that Twitter
doesn't work; it's that most brands aren't using Twitter correctly. It's like saying that a trumpet is broken
because the first hundred people who try to play it
suck. You can't have a relationship with someone
if you won't shut up and let him or her get a word
in edgewise. Brands have to realize that it's not all
about them. When they do nothing but push product, there's no reason for the consumer to say anything back. It's like that friend you have who always
talks about herself and never asks how you're doing.
Eventually, she gets tiresome, and you lose interest in
keeping up the friendship.

2. "Brands only engage 18%." Well, whose fault is that?

3. Twitter is four years old, and we should treat it like
   any four-year-old. Give it a little time to grow up and
   mature before dismissing it.

Getting Started

You don't have to be Michael Phelps, but for God's sake, put on
a bathing suit!

Jeff Bezos's Missed Opportunity

Bezos bought two of the few companies that have most interested
me—Zappos and Woot. Woot.com is a site that sells one cool, dis-

counted electronic item per day. When the item runs out, the sale is over, and everyone has to wait until midnight of the following day, Central Time, to see what new awesome thing is on the market. When Woot launched in 2004, I said, "Shoot, I should have built that! I soooo get it!" It's the site that inspired me to branch out of wine retail. Amazon bought it in June 2010, but it should have bought the company three or four years ago. I'm a little surprised that it took Bezos so long to see Woot's potential, since the single-option, restrictive buying trend seemed so obvious. And I am really disappointed in myself for not taking action and launching a startup around the same idea. I made a half-assed effort with a site called Free.WineLibrary.com, but it didn't take off. It took me until 2009 to get the formula right with Cinderella Wine. Kudos to the founders of Groupon and Living Social for running headfirst into the opportunity and executing so successfully.

Apologies

LeBron James was apparently counting on the public's capacity for forgiveness when he decided it would be a good idea to announce on live national television that he was dumping his hometown team, the Cleveland Cavaliers, to play for the Miami Heat. Talk about stabbing the people that love you in the back! Still, Cleveland will probably eventually forgive him. But if he were smart, he'd have taken note of his fans' anger, put together another live TV appearance, and say, "I had my reasons for going to Miami, but Cleveland, I've been a jerk, and I'm sorry." And if his handlers or agents had been smart, they would have been watching Twitter while LeBron made his announcement, seen the public reaction, given him a talking-to during a commercial break, and allowed him to express his regret on the spot for upsetting so many people. That would have been news! In any scenario, however, his apology would have to be genuine. There's never a time when real doesn't work.

Hiring and Firing

I value good teamwork more than almost anything. Though I rarely fire anyone, over the years I've had to let go of five of the most talented employees that have ever worked at Wine Library, because they just couldn't play nice with the other boys and girls. That was culturally unacceptable in my company.

Leadership and Culture

Bill Parcells is the best coach of all time. Screw Phil Jackson— I could have won a few championships with Jordan, Shaq, and Kobe on my teams. Parcells is the greatest coach in history because he went to a rotten New York Giants team and won two Super Bowls; went to the New York Jets, who had won four games in two years, and in two short years got them within one game of the Super Bowl; went to the Patriots, who were one in fifteen, and took them to the Super Bowl; went to Dallas and made them a consistent playoffs contender; and then to Miami, where he coached the biggest turnaround in one season in NFL history. He wins through building team morale, hiring the right people, and instilling the right culture. He brings his DNA. In this new world where people can communicate more freely with not just customers, but with employees too, the Bill Parcells style of leadership will become more and more necessary.

Talent

Companies that resist the Thank You Economy are going to see an exodus of talent. The people who understand where the culture is going but don't get support from their companies are going to find the courage to leave for new pastures. In communist societies, people resist covertly. They're suppressed; they fight the system; and as soon as they can, they leave.

One day these companies are going to realize that they have to get on board. They're going to look internally for the leaders to take them there and execute, and find that the people they need bailed out of frustration a few years earlier. They didn't appreciate what they had until it was too late.

Communism in Corporate America

The economy and our culture are inextricably linked, to the point that, in my mind, they are one and the same. If you understand the culture we're in right now, you understand that there's nothing an employee can say that will irreparably damage your business, especially if you fix it quickly. That's what capitalism understands and communism doesn't.

Tony Hsieh's Letter to His Employees

When Amazon acquired Zappos, even the way the acquisition was announced was culturally significant. Tony Hsieh, CEO of

Zappos, wrote an incredibly personal letter to Zappos employees explaining the details of the transaction, what it meant for the company, and how it would affect their jobs.

Date: Wed, 22 Jul 2009
From: Tony Hsieh (CEO—Zappos.com)
To: All Zappos Employees
Subject: Zappos and Amazon

Please set aside 20 minutes to carefully read this entire email. (My apologies for the occasional use of formal-sounding language, as parts of it are written in a particular way for legal reasons.)

Today is a big day in Zappos history.

This morning, our board approved and we signed what's known as a "definitive agreement," in which all of the existing shareholders and investors of Zappos (there are over 100) will be exchanging their Zappos stock for Amazon stock. Once the exchange is done, Amazon will become the only shareholder of Zappos stock.

Over the next few days, you will probably read headlines that say "Amazon acquires Zappos" or "Zappos sells to Amazon." While those headlines are technically correct, they don't really properly convey the spirit of the transaction. (I personally would prefer the headline "Zappos and Amazon sitting in a tree . . .")

We plan to continue to run Zappos the way we have always run Zappos—continuing to do what we believe is best for our brand, our culture, and our business. From a practical point of view, it will be as if we are switching out our current shareholders and board of directors for a new one, even though the technical legal structure may be different.

We think that now is the right time to join forces with Amazon because there is a huge opportunity to leverage each other's strengths and move even faster towards our long term vision. For Zappos, our vision remains the same: delivering happiness to customers, employees, and vendors. We just want to get there faster.

We are excited about doing this for 3 main reasons:

1) We think that there is a huge opportunity for us to really accelerate the growth of the Zappos brand and culture, and we believe that Amazon is the best partner to help us get there faster.

2) Amazon supports us in continuing to grow our vision as an independent entity, under the Zappos brand and with our unique culture.

3) We want to align ourselves with a shareholder and partner that thinks really long term (like we do at Zappos), as well as do what's in the best interest of our existing shareholders and investors.

I will go through each of the above points in more detail below, but first, let me get to the top 3 burning questions that I'm guessing many of you will have.

TOP 3 BURNING QUESTIONS

Q: Will I still have a job?

As mentioned above, we plan to continue to run Zappos

as an independent entity. In legal terminology, Zappos will be a "wholly-owned subsidiary" of Amazon. Your job is just as secure as it was a month ago.

Q: Will the Zappos culture change?

Our culture at Zappos is unique and always evolving and changing, because one of our core values is to Embrace and Drive Change. What happens to our culture is up to us, which has always been true. Just like before, we are in control of our destiny and how our culture evolves.

A big part of the reason why Amazon is interested in us is because they recognize the value of our culture, our people, and our brand. Their desire is for us to continue to grow and develop our culture (and perhaps even a little bit of our culture may rub off on them).

They are not looking to have their folks come in and run Zappos unless we ask them to. That being said, they have a lot of experience and expertise in a lot of areas, so we're very excited about the opportunities to tap into their knowledge, expertise, and resources, especially on the technology side. This is about making the Zappos brand, culture, and business even stronger than it is today.

Q: Are Tony, Alfred, or Fred leaving?

No, we have no plans to leave. We believe that we are at the very beginning of what's possible for Zappos and are very excited about the future and what we can accomplish for Zappos with Amazon as our new partner. Part of the reason for doing this is so that we can get a lot more done more quickly.

There is an additional Q&A section at the end of this

email, but I wanted to make sure we got the top 3 burning questions out of the way first. Now that we've covered those questions, I wanted to share in more detail our thinking behind the scenes that led us to this decision.

First, I want to apologize for the suddenness of this announcement. As you know, one of our core values is to Build Open and Honest Relationships With Communication, and if I could have it my way, I would have shared much earlier that we were in discussions with Amazon so that all employees could be involved in the decision process that we went through along the way. Unfortunately, because Amazon is a public company, there are securities laws that prevented us from talking about this to most of our employees until today.

We've been on friendly terms with Amazon for many years, as they have always been interested in Zappos and have always had a great respect for our brand.

Several months ago, they reached out to us and said they wanted to join forces with us so that we could accelerate the growth of our business, our brand, and our culture. When they said they wanted us to continue to build the Zappos brand (as opposed to folding us into Amazon), we decided it was worth exploring what a partnership would look like.

We learned that they truly wanted us to continue to build the Zappos brand and continue to build the Zappos culture in our own unique way. (I think "unique" was their way of saying "fun and a little weird." :)

Over the past several months, as we got to know each other better, both sides became more and more excited about the possibilities for leveraging each other's strengths.

We realized that we are both very customer-focused companies—we just focus on different ways of making our customers happy.

Amazon focuses on low prices, vast selection and convenience to make their customers happy, while Zappos does it through developing relationships, creating personal emotional connections, and delivering high touch ("WOW") customer service.

We realized that Amazon's resources, technology, and operational experience had the potential to greatly accelerate our growth so that we could grow the Zappos brand and culture even faster. On the flip side, through the process Amazon realized that it really was the case that our culture is the platform that enables us to deliver the Zappos experience to our customers. Jeff Bezos (CEO of Amazon) made it clear that he had a great deal of respect for our culture and that Amazon would look to protect it.

We asked our board members what they thought of the opportunity. Michael Moritz, who represents Sequoia Capital (one of our investors and board members), wrote the following: "You now have the opportunity to accelerate Zappos' progress and to make the name and the brand and everything associated with it an enduring, permanent part of peoples' lives . . . You are now free to let your imagination roam—and to contemplate initiatives and undertakings that today, in our more constrained setting, we could not take on."

One of the great things about Amazon is that they are very long term thinkers, just like we are at Zappos. Alignment in very long term thinking is hard to find in a partner or investor, and we felt very lucky and excited to learn that both Amazon and Zappos shared this same philosophy.

All this being said, this was not an easy decision. Over the past several months, we had to weigh all the pros and cons along with all the potential benefits and risks. At the end of the day, we realized that, once it was determined that this was in the best interests of our shareholders, it basically all boiled down to asking ourselves 2 questions:

1) Do we believe that this will accelerate the growth of the Zappos brand and help us fulfill our mission of delivering happiness faster?

2) Do we believe that we will continue to be in control of our own destiny so that we can continue to grow our unique culture?

After spending a lot of time with Amazon and getting to know them and understanding their intentions better, we reached the conclusion that the answers to these 2 questions are YES and YES.

The Zappos brand will continue to be separate from the Amazon brand. Although we'll have access to many of Amazon's resources, we need to continue to build our brand and our culture just as we always have. Our mission remains the same: delivering happiness to all of our stakeholders, including our employees, our customers, and our vendors. (As a side note, we plan to continue to maintain the relationships that we have with our vendors ourselves, and Amazon will continue to maintain the relationships that they have with their vendors.)

We will be holding an all hands meeting soon to go over all of this in more detail. Please email me any questions that you may have so that we can cover as many as possible during the all hands meeting and/or a follow-up email.

We signed what's known as the "definitive agreement" today, but we still need to go through the process of getting government approval, so we are anticipating that this transaction actually won't officially close for at least a few months. We are legally required by the SEC to be in what's known as a "quiet period," so if you get any questions related to the transaction from anyone including customers, vendors, or the media, please let them know that we are in a quiet period mandated by law and have them email tree@zappos.com, which is a special email account that Alfred and I will be monitoring.

Alfred and I would like to say thanks to the small group of folks on our finance and legal teams and from our advisors at Morgan Stanley, Fenwick & West, and PricewaterhouseCoopers who have been working really hard, around the clock, and behind the scenes over the last several months to help make all this possible.

Before getting to the Q&A section, I'd also like to thank everyone for taking the time to read this long email and for helping us get to where we are today.

It's definitely an emotional day for me. The feelings I'm experiencing are similar to what I felt in college on graduation day: excitement about the future mixed with fond memories of the past. The last 10 years were an incredible ride, and I'm excited about what we will accomplish together over the next 10 years as we continue to grow Zappos!

—Tony Hsieh

CEO—Zappos.com

Compare this letter to some of the stiff, jargon-filled letters most CEOs send out to their companies when they make big announcements. They may as well have been written by HAL, from *2001: A Space Odyssey*, for all the genuine personality, compassion, and concern they project. Very few employees feel safe after receiving one of those, yet I imagine that most of the Zappos staff who read Hsieh's letter believed that the decisions made on behalf of the company were made with the right intent. And good intent, as we've discussed, goes a long, long way.

How Innovation Feeds Culture

You can never lose by going out on a creative limb. Even if your campaign doesn't result in the sales you might have hoped for, your company culture will benefit from having tried. Talent wants to follow talent. Any creative team who sees that you tried something innovative will keep you in mind when they're ready to job hunt.

Choosing a Community Manager

Put the best people in charge of social media, not the people you don't know what else to do with. Teams don't pick the chubby, out-of-shape guy first if they want to win; you shouldn't pick the second-rate player to do something that requires smarts, empathy, and flexibility.

Viral Ping-Pong

People like surprises. When somebody who is known for his or her television or film appearances shows up on Diggnation, a popular video blog, or starts tweeting great content, it becomes noteworthy; it's like suddenly getting a peek inside the head of someone you've always wanted to get to know better. It can work the other way, too.

If Hallmark ran a TV commercial for Mother's Day and featured a bunch of popular online characters and their moms, like Kevin Rose, iJustine, and Tony Hsieh—or if these Web celebrities did a "Got Milk" print campaign—I'm sure the ads would go crazy viral. Seeing those personalities on television or in print would take the public by as much surprise as if they saw a fish walking down the street. There are a lot of impressions to be made if brands would take advantage of the reciprocal relationships between traditional and social media.

The Interplay between Traditional and Social Media

There's still a perception that traditional media works—that people see it—and social media doesn't. What a lot of people fail to realize is how much traditional media is seen because of social media. The 2010 Grammys experienced a 35 percent hike in viewership since 2009, and was the most watched Grammys event since 2004. Credit could be given to the stellar mainstream lineup, or an increase in country fans, or various promotions, but I'm sure social media had something to do with it, too. When

@KatoriHall
Katori Hall

Pink at the Grammys absolutely
PHENOMENAL!!! Now THAT'S a
performer

31 Jan via TweetDeck   ☆ Favorite ⇄ Retweet ↩ Reply

@courtney_chow
Courtney Chow

Drake… you da you da besttt! & Pink was
beyond amazing <3 #grammys

1 Feb via web   ☆ Favorite ⇄ Retweet ↩ Reply

Pink started spinning, wet and nearly naked, in a Cirque du Soleil–style harness while singing "Glitter in the Sky," Twitter went nuts, leading people to think, "Huh, maybe I should tune in."

People who weren't planning to watch the Grammys saw that their friends were watching the Grammys and saw that there was some crazy stuff going on at the Grammys, and tuned in. We used to do that. We'd be watching something awesome on TV and pick up the phone and say, did you see that? If we were super advanced, we might have three-way calling and be able to talk to two friends at the same time! But what were we going to do then—hang up, dial another friend, and another? Of course not! With one click, we now can tell everyone we know to get their butts in front of the TV before they miss the awesome show.

Tactics

Intent will make your tactics work better. Your re-tweet tactic will work really well if you care like crazy for a year before you try the tactic, and even better if what you do isn't really a tactic at all; it's just what you do. It's like when you're nice to someone and then you ask the person a favor . . . that person is a lot more likely to do something for you if you've been a great friend and neighbor than if you've ignored him or her the whole time you've lived next door to each other.

I use tactics, too, but my engagements far, far outnumber them. Tactics are like dessert. Dessert is great unless you eat it with every meal, every day.

Earned Media

In the spring of 2010, Vaynermedia facilitated a campaign between the New Jersey Nets and the geo-location site Gowalla. The goal was to raise brand awareness and bring more fans to the games. The Nets dropped 250 pairs of virtual tickets around sports venues, including sports bars and gyms, near the Nets' arena in New York and New Jersey; anyone who checked in with Gowalla could find the tickets and redeem them for real ones to the final home game of the season. Virtual merchandise that could be redeemed for real team memorabilia would also be awarded to people who checked in at the game.

Business insiders wrote that the Gowalla campaign was a failure because only 15.2 percent of the Gowalla winners made it to the game, but they were mistaken. First of all, we knew there would be challenges to getting people in the seats: the Nets had had a lousy season, the game was on a Monday night, and the arena is extremely hard to get to via public transportation, which is the only way many New Yorkers travel. Given those obstacles, a 15.2 percent conversion rate wasn't too bad. Second, what the critics didn't realize is that by writing about the campaign, even if only to criticize, they made it work by extending the story. It also got a lot of positive attention from ESPN and bloggers. Last, the participants themselves had a great time and helped make the campaign work. Their numbers may have been small, but many of them tweeted and sent photos of the event throughout the evening, and continued talking about their experience for days after the game.

Some people suggested that Gowalla might have gotten something out of the campaign, but not the Nets. The Nets did enjoy added business, though, and on top of that, they could now claim to be a brand that's willing to push creative boundaries. Only "B"-playing businesspeople would look at that campaign and dismiss it as a waste of time. Forward-thinking, creative individuals saw the initiative and thought, "There's a brand I want to work with." People who care only about the numbers often miss the most interesting part of the story. In the end, Gowalla and the Nets each got exactly what they wanted from the campaign.

Squeaky Wheels

Some people recognize that in these early days of social media, complaining will get them some attention. It can be frustrating to interact with these squeaky wheels, especially when you suspect they're just trying to get attention or free stuff or to hear themselves talk, but you have to take the high road. You can't ignore these people; you have to care, no matter what. That said, you have to be a good judge of when it's time to move on.

The Biggest Mistakes Companies Make with Social Media

1. Using tactics instead of strategy
2. Using it exclusively to put out fires
3. Using it to brag
4. Using it as a press release
5. Exclusively re-tweeting other people's material rather than creating your own original content
6. Using it to push product
7. Expecting immediate results

Anyone Who Cares About Legacy Must Take the TYE Seriously

Mr. Buffett, if you want everything you've built to last long after you're gone, make sure that your companies are introducing Thank You Economy sensibility into their business practices. Actually, any investor would do well to heed the same advice. If you've inherited a family business and you want it to be strong for generations to come, it's up to you to start shaking things up and instilling TYE culture from the top.

Fish the Small Ponds

Facebook is not the only significant social media platform, but many people think they have to fish in the big ocean and ignore the pond. The ponds are rich sources of revenue. Before we launched Vaynermedia, AJ and I were going to start a fantasy sports site. Had we chosen that path, we probably would have spent much of our money on Facebook ads, but we also would have spent countless hours engaging in the fifty most prominent fantasy sports blogs and forums. They wouldn't have had as many eyeballs as Facebook, but those eyeballs would have been a committed, dedicated potential audience. It is time for companies to allocate to the ponds some of the money they're pouring into the big oceans.

Why Big Companies Focus on Big Platforms

Right now in big companies there are four people or perhaps six people on staff making decisions with a $40 million budget. They spend their money on agencies, bringing in consultants, paying outside people to come in and execute their campaigns. Of course they have to focus on the big platforms—they need a huge payoff to justify all the money they're spending. So what you hear in these meetings is "Let's get this one platform right before we do the next one."

It's going to take a lot more people. You can't have just one person flying a plane and dropping sixty bombs; you need a lot of people on the ground going one-on-one. Businesses have to quit outsourcing everything and start building up their internal teams around these new platforms.

Why People Respond to Social Media

I'm not saying that business leaders don't know how to run their own businesses; I'm saying that they can do an even better job. Eventually, the marketing shifts that merely give them an advantage now are going to be prerequisites for success. We connect on a human level, and consumers are going to expect that kind of connection when they deal with you. A lot of people who have been in the hospital will complain that they sometimes didn't see their doctor for days, and then when she came in she was aloof and academic and studied her patient like an interesting case, not a human being with feelings. It's the nurses that often make people feel better when they're in the hospital. When patients leave, they're often eternally grateful to the doctor or surgeon who saved their life or made them feel better, but they often hold deep-felt affection and gratitude to the nurses who brought them extra pillows and took the time to explain things, who altered their regular shifts to make sure they were on the floor when their patient came back from a procedure. When these people talk about their experience, they'll recommend the doctor, but they'll rave about the hospital nurse and the care they received. They needed the doctor for her expertise; they loved the nurse for her compassion and care. Brands that win in the Thank You Economy will figure out how to provide both—what consumers need *and* what they want.

PART V

How to Win in the Thank You Economy, the Quick Version

- Care—about your customers, about your employees, about your brand—with everything you've got.
- Erase any lines in the sand—don't be afraid of what's new or unfamiliar.
- Show up first to market whenever possible, early the rest of the time.
- Instill a culture of caring into your business by:
    Being self-aware
    Mentally committing to change
    Setting the tone through your words and actions
    Investing in your employees
    Hiring culturally compatible DNA, and spotting it within your existing team
    Being authentic—whether online or offline, say what you mean, and mean what you say
    Empowering your people to be forthright, creative, and generous
- Remember that behind every B2B transaction, there is a C.
- Speak your customers' language.
- Allow your customers to help you shape your brand or business, but never allow them to dictate the direction in which you take it.
- Build a sense of community around your brand.

- Arrange for traditional and social media to play Ping-Pong and extend every conversation.
- Direct all of your marketing initiatives toward the emotional center, and to the creative extremes.
- Approach social media initiatives with good intent, aiming for quality engagements, not quantity.
- Use shock and awe to blow your customers' minds and get them talking.
- If you must use tactics, use "pull" tactics that remind consumers why they should care about your brand.
- If you're small, play like you're big; if you're big, play like you're small.
- Create a sense of community around your business or your brand.
- Don't be afraid to crawl before you run.

PSSSSSST!

Hey . . .

Thank you for reading. Here is my email: gary@vaynermedia.com. Let me know if I can be of help.

NOTES

9 **A survey of parents:** W. David Gardner, "Facebook, Twitter Influence Purchases," InformationWeek.com, July 27, 2010. http://www.informationweek.com/news/software/web_services/showArticle.jhtml?articleID=226300075.

9 **another survey, conducted in early December 2009:** Bilal Hameed, "Facebook, Twitter Influences Up to 28% of Online Decisions," StartupMeme.com, December 14, 2009. http://startupmeme.com/facebook-twitter-influences-up-to-28-of-online-buying-decisions.

10 **Meanwhile, at its peak:** Eric Caoili, "Farmville Sheds Another 9 Million Users in Latest Facebook Rankings," Gamasutra, June 10, 2010. http://www.gamasutra.com/view/news/28913/FarmVille_Sheds_Another_9_Million_Users_In_Latest_Facebook_Rankings.php.

15 **As the 1980s rolled into the 1990s:** Emily Yellin, *Your Call Is (Not That) Important to Us* (New York: The Free Press, 2009). 80–81.

16 **In the event they could dig up a phone number:** Yellin, 73–74.

21 **According to Facebook:** Rick Burnes, "Twitter User Growth Slowed from Peak of 13% in March 2009 to 3.5% in October," Hubspot Blog, January 19, 2010. http://blog.hubspot.com/blog/tabid/6307/bid/5496/Twitter-User-Growth-Slowed-From-Peak-of-13-in-March-2009-to-3-5-in-October.aspx.

23 **In reply, Galante received a voice mail:** Nilay Patel, "AT&T Warns Customer That Emailing the CEO Will Result in a Cease and Desist Letter," Engadget.com, June 2, 2010. http://www.engadget.com/2010/06/02/atandt-warns-customer-that-emailing-the-ceo-will-result-in-a-cease.

23 **He finally received (and accepted) an apology:** Giorgio Galante, *So Long and Thanks for All the Fish.* http://attepicfail.tumblr.com.

23 **If there were a particularly juicy angle to the story:** Yellin, 5.

28 **Even industries that have long resisted:** Jeremy W. Peters, "Some Newspapers, Tracking Readers Online, Shift Coverage," *New York Times*, September 5, 2010. http://www.nytimes.com/2010/09/06/business/media/06track.html?_r=1&emc=eta1.

30   **What's extra special about the Wufoo notes:** Examples of Wufoo cards: Drew McClellan, "Marketing Tip #75: Handwritten Notes Are Magic, *Drew's Marketing Minute,* July 14, 2010, http://www.drewsmarketing minute.com/2010/07/marketing-tip-75-handwritten-notes-are-magic .html. Also see Gene, "Wufoo Loves Their Customers," *Period Three Blog,* March 13, 2009. http://blog.period-three.com/2009/03/13/wufoo-loves-their-customers/.

36   **They choose to invest in innovation:** Julia Kirby, "Wall Street Is No Friend to Radical Innovation," *US Airways Magazine,* July 2010, 17–18.

38   **Though girls ages fourteen to seventeen can still out-text anyone:** Shane Snow, "The Rise of Text Messaging," Mashable.com, August 2010. http:// mashable.com/2010/08/17/text-messaging-infographic/.

38   **As of May 2010:** Amanda Lenhart, "Cell Phones and American Adults," Pew Internet and American Life Project, September 2, 2010. http://www .pewinternet.org/Reports/2010/Cell-Phones-and-American-Adults/Over view.aspx.

39   **Over the next two decades:** Nina and Tim Zagat, "Nina and Tim Zagat," Slate.com, June 1, 1999. http://www.slate.com/id/29583/entry/29585.

39   **The decidedly hip site:** Heather Maddan, "Casting the Net," SFGate.com, June 18, 2006. http://www.sfgate.com/cgi-bin/article.cgi?f=/c/a/2006/06/18/ LVGO9JDMDv1.DTL&hw=yelp&sn=001&sc=1000.

39   **Yelp reports five million unique visitors:** Yelp.com, Press Page, "Company Announcements." http://www.yelp.com/press/announcements.

39   **The Zagats try to sell their business:** Paul Tharp, "Zagat-about-'em," NY Post.com, September 8, 2009. http://www.nypost.com/p/news/business/za-gat_about_em_FyHeEMEeS2WHoNCUhv1UAK.

39   **Yelp reports ten million unique visitors:** Yelp.com.

40   **The Zagats take the business off the market:** Tharp, "Zagat-about-'em."

40   **Zagat holds steady as one of the top ten iPhone apps:** Jillian Reagan, "Za-gat Me, Baby!," *The New York Observer,* July 7, 2009. http://www.observer .com/2009/media/zagat-me-baby-new-mobile-app-will-tell-you-where-eat.

40   **Yelp, which is still free:** Yelp.com.

40   **Zagat.com, which charges a $25 annual membership fee:** Tharp, "Zagat-about-'em."

40   **"Yelp has the chance":** Peter Burrows, "Hot Tech Companies Like Yelp Are Bypassing IPOs," Businessweek.com, February 2010. http://www.business week.com/magazine/content/10_07/b4166023271880.htm.

40   **Modeling Foursquare, Yelp adds:** John C. Abell, "Yelp Takes on Four-square in latest iPhone App Upgrade," Wired.com, January 19, 2010. http:// www.wired.com/epicenter/2010/01/yelp-iphone-foursquare.

40   **Foursquare users can earn a "Foodie badge":** Jenna Wortham, "Four-square Signs a Deal with Zagat," *New York Times,* February 9, 2010. http:// bits.blogs.nytimes.com/2010/02/09/foursquare-inks-a-deal-with-zagat.

41   **Zagat Integrates Foodspotting:** Zagat.com, Press Center. http://www .zagat.com/About/Index.aspx?menu=PR192.

47 **Every time a seismic shift:** Joshua Cooper Ramo, "Why the Founder of Amazon Is Our Choice for 1999," *Time*, December 1999.

51 **"Most Brands Still Irrelevant on Twitter":** Michael Learmonth, "Study: Most Brands Still Irrelevant on Twitter," AdAge.com, July 27, 2010. http://adage.com/digital/article?article_id=145107.

51 **"Social Networking May Not Be":** Charles Hugh Smith, "Social Networking May Not Be as Profitable as Many Think," DailyFinance.com, July 20, 2010. http://www.dailyfinance.com/story/media/social-networking-may-not-be-as-profitable-as-many-think/19560291.

53 **When Nielsen conducted a study:** "Friending the Social Consumer," Nielsen Wire, June 16, 2010. http://blog.nielsen.com/nielsenwire/online_mobile/friending-the-social-consumer.

55 **According to an IBM study:** Maureen Stancik Boyce and Laura VanTyne, "Why Advocacy Matters to Online Retailers," IBM Institute for Business Value Distribution, November 18, 2008.

55 Blackshaw deck, "Are Consumers Willing to Engage and Be Spokespeople for Our Brands?," 2.

56 Blackshaw deck, "Loyalty Is No Longer Enough," 3.

56 Ibid.

56 **According to Jason Mittelstaedt:** Lora Kolodny, "Study: 82% of U.S. Consumers Bail on Brands After Bad Customer Service," TechCrunch, October 13, 2010. http://techcrunch.com/2010/10/13/customer-service-rightnow.

56 Blackshaw deck, "Are Consumers Willing to Engage and Be Spokespeople for Our Brands?," 3.

58 **In the press release, Steve Hasker:** "Nielsen Unveils New Online Advertising Measurement," News Releases, Nielsen.com. http://en-us.nielsen.com/content/nielsen/en_us/news/news_releases/2010/september/nielsen_unveils_newonlineadvertisingmeasurement.html.

59 **In 2010, *Adweek* reported that Vitrue:** Brian Morrissey, "Value of a 'Fan' on Social Media: $3.60," Adweek.com, April 13, 2010. http://www.adweek.com/aw/content_display/news/digital/e3iaf69ea67183512325a8feefb9f969530.

65 **It wasn't until 1922:** "KDKA Begins to Broadcast 1920," *A Science Odyssey: People and Discoveries*, PBS.org, http://www.pbs.org/wgbh/aso/databank/entries/dt20ra.html.

66 http://www.adi-news.com/comscore-twitter-overtaken-myspace-for-the-third-spot-among-social-networking-site-facebook-still-on-top/25263.

68 **To prove them wrong:** Leslie Goldman, "Ann Taylor LOFT Ditches Models for Real Women," iVillage.com, June 21, 2010. http://www.ivillage.com/ann-taylor-loft-ditches-models-real-women/4-a–213041.

68 **"I love LOFT and I soooo appreciate":** LOFT, "How LOFT Is Wearing Our Favorite New Pant," Facebook, last updated around July 2010. http://www.facebook.com/album.php?aid=183697&id=26483215676.

96 **She then wrote an entire blog post:** www.rachel-levy.com/music-and-the-impact-of-a-tweet.

98   **"Ben, first of all, thanks for your note":** "This CEO Sucks Less: John Pepper of Boloco," The Consumerist.com, January 25, 2006. http://consumerist
.com/2006/01/this-ceo-sucks-less-john-pepper-of-boloco.html.

105   **"I say many times":** John Paul Morosi, "Joyce, Galarraga Make Up After Blown Call in Near-Perfect Game," June 3, 2010, FOXsports.com. http://
msn.foxsports.com/mlb/story/Jim-Joyce-Armando-Galarraga-make-up-after-blown-call–060310.

105   **As was to be expected:** Tom Verduci with Melissa Segura, "A Different Kind of Perfect," SIVault, SportsIllustrated.com, June 14, 2010. http://sports
illustrated.cnn.com/vault/article/magazine/MAG1170587/3/index.htm.

105   **By the next day:** Ibid.

106   **Only a few weeks:** "Joyce Tops Survey; Players Nix Replay," ESPN.com, June 13, 2010. http://sports.espn.go.com/mlb/news/story?id=5281467.

123   **For example, sales of Old Spice Body Wash:** Noreen O'Leary and Todd Wasserman, "Old Spice Campaign Smells Like a Sales Success, Too," Brand
week.com, July 25, 2010. http://www.brandweek.com/bw/content_display/
news-and-features/direct/e3i45f1c709df0501927f56568a2acd5c7b.

123   **but some seem to question:** Joseph Jaffe, "Sugar and Old Spice," Adweek.com, July 27, 2010. http://www.adweek.com/aw/content_display/community/
columns/other-columns/e3i45f1c709df050192d35f3e8e86cc5a79.

126   *Ad Age* **published an article:** Edmund Lee, "Old Spice Fades Into History While Samsung, Ikea, Twitter Scale Viral Chart," AdAge.com, September 23, 2010. http://adage.com/digital/article?article_id=146030.

142   **When YouTube user Pierce Ruane:** "Rapper 50 Cent Invites Dorky YouTube Fan 'Sexman' to NYC to Hang Out," Gawkk.com. http://www.gawkk
.com/in-nyc-with-50-cent/discuss.

147   **According to MailerMailer's metrics report:** Anthony Schneider, "Open Rates and Click Rates Are Declining," Email Transmit Info Center, July 29, 2010. http://infocenter.emailtransmit.com/2010/07/open-rates-and-click-rates-are-declining.

148   **They have also changed:** "Web banner," Wikipedia. http://en.wikipedia
.org/wiki/Banner_ad.

148   **At that time, banner ads:** Frank D'Angelo, "Happy Birthday, Digital Advertising!" AdvertisingAge.com, October 26, 2009. http://adage.com/digital
next/article?article_id=139964.

148   **Today, banner ad CTR:** Dirk Singer, "Happy Birthday Banner Ad . . . Bet You Wish Click Through Rates Were Still 78%." http://liesdamnedlies
statistics.com/category/click-through-rate.

153   **Over 60 percent of Americans:** Andrea Larrumbide, "Cone Finds That Americans Expect Companies to Have a Presence in Social Media," Cone Inc., September 25, 2008. http://www.coneinc.com/content1182.

153   **for example, Burger King estimates:** Erik Qualman, "Social Media ROI: Socialnomics," YouTube. http://www.youtube.com/watch?v=ypmfs3z8esI&
feature=player_embedded#!

159   **In the restaurant world:** Kerry Miller, "The Restaurant-Failure Myth,"

Businessweek.com, April 16, 2007. http://www.businessweek.com/smallbiz/content/apr2007/sb20070416_296932.htm.

161   **A flash mob of 161 Foursquare users:** Pamela Seiple, "Restaurant Owner Increases Sales by 110% with Foursquare Swarm Badge Party, Hubspot Blog, March 8, 2010. http://blog.hubspot.com/blog/tabid/6307/bid/5697/Restaurant-Owner-Increases-Sales-by-110-with-Foursquare-Swarm-Badge-Party.aspx.

161   **At the time of the swarm event:** Ibid.

163   **"This restaurant in particular":** Augie Ray, "Word of Mouth and Social Media: A Tale of Two Burger Joints," Augie Ray's Blog, March 28, 2010. http://blogs.forrester.com/augie_ray/10-03-28-word_mouth_and_social_media_tale_two_burger_joints.

173   **For example, while any staff member:** Kathryn M. Kantes, "Joie de Vivre and the Art of the Hotel," Hospitality.net, March 5, 2010. http://www.hospitalitynet.org/news/4045696.search?query=joie+de+vivre%2c+dream+maker%2c+word+of+mouth.

178   **According to a 2009 Pew Research Center report:** Pew Research Center, "61% of American adults look online for health information," Pew Research Center press release, PewInternet.org, June 11, 2009. http://www.pewinternet.org/Press-Releases/2009/The-Social-Life-of-Health-Information.aspx.

182   **But Loïc Le Meur is very interested:** BusinessWeek Tech Team, "The 25 Most Influential People on the Web," BusinessWeek.com, September 2008. http://images.businessweek.com/ss/08/09/0929_most_influential/1.htm.

183   **You can see:** Loïc Le Meur, "Does My Dentist Really Need a Facebook Fan Page, You Tube Channel, and a Twitter Account?", Loïc Le Meur, July 9, 2010. http://www.loiclemeur.com/english/2010/07/does-my-dentist-really-need-a-facebook-fan-page-youtube-channel-and-a-twitter-account.html?utm_source=feedburner&utm_medium=feed&utm_campaign=Feed%3A+loiclemeur+%28Loic+Le+Meur+Blog%29.

183   **From there, TechCrunch picked up the story:** Leena Rao, "How Social Media Drives New Business: Six Case Studies," TechCrunch, July 17, 2010. http://techcrunch.com/2010/07/17/how-social-media-drives-new-business-six-case-studies.

188   **While the new crop of law school graduates:** John Schwartz, "A Legal Battle: Online Attitude vs. Rules of the Bar," *New York Times*, September 12, 2009. http://www.nytimes.com/2009/09/13/us/13lawyers.html?_r=1&hp.

188   **Even attorneys who know their stuff:** Ibid.

202   **In an article for the *Nieman Journalism Lab*:** Justin Ellis, "Twitter Data Lets NPR Glimpse a Future of App-Loving News Junkies," Nieman Journalism Lab, October 8, 2010. http://www.niemanlab.org/2010/10/twitter-data-lets-npr-glimpse-a-future-of-app-loving-news-junkies.

207   **Selecting for demographics:** Lyn Schafer Gross, "Ratings," The Museum of Broadcast Communications. http://www.museum.tv/eotvsection.php?entrycode=ratings.

207   **In 2009, there were about 114,900,000:** "114.9 Million U.S. Television

Homes Estimated for 2009–2010 Season," Nielsen Wire, August 29, 2009. http://blog.nielsen.com/nielsenwire/media_entertainment/1149-million-us-television-homes-estimated-for-2009-2010-season.

207 **Of those households:** "TV Ratings," Nielsen.com. http://en-us.nielsen.com/content/nielsen/en_us/measurement/tv_research/tv_ratings.html.

207 **The sample does get broader:** Gross, "Ratings."

207 **A quick search on the Internet:** There are many confessions to pick from: Christopher Lawrence, "Life on the Couch: Being a Nielsen family serious business," *Las Vegas Review Journal*, March 22, 2009. http://www.lvrj.com/living/41647782.html; "The Nielsens," "Confessions of a Nielsen Family," *New York Daily News*. http://www.frankwbaker.com/nielsenconfessions.htm; Anonymous, "My Life as a Nielsen Family," *Slate*, July 15, 1997. http://www.slate.com/id/3809/entry/24393/; James C. Raymondo and Horst Stipp, "Confessions of a Nielsen Household," *American Demographics*, March 1997. http://findarticles.com/p/articles/mi_m4021/is_n3_v19/ai_19165304/pg_2/; and Mary Beth Ellis, "Confessions of a Nielsen Viewer," MSNBC.com, March 27, 2006. http://today.msnbc.msn.com/id/11716703.

207 **In 2009, the company released a report:** Michael Schneider, "Fox Wants Answers from Nielsen," Variety.com, May 18, 2009. http://www.variety.com/article/VR111800392,4.html?categoryid=14&cs=1http://www.variety.com/article/VR1118003924.html?categoryid=14&cs=1.

208 **Nielsen issued a 2010 report:** "Americans Using TV and Internet Together 35% More than a Year Ago," March 22, 2010. http://blog.nielsen.com/nielsenwire/online_mobile/three-screen-report-q409.

208 **In the 1940s and '50s:** Television Obscurities, Nielsen "Black Weeks," February 9, 2009. http://www.tvobscurities.com/articles/nielsen_black_weeks.php.

208 **it was common for television series producers:** Jim Cox, *Sold on Radio* (North Carolina: McFarland, 2008). 46. http://books.google.com/books?id=RwVkMMLqMdkC&pg=PA46&lpg=PA46&dq=%22How%27s+your+Hooper%3F%22&source=bl&ots=qUfAze9xT0&sig=GNOC0Q7nTJ4gILmjquxsJPdRboU&hl=en&ei=pQOhTKL-N4L88AbZmsyNAw&sa=X&oi=book_result&ct=result&resnum=5&ved=0CCYQ6AEwBA#v=onepageq=%22How%27s%20your%20Hooper%3F%22&f=falsehttp://en.wikipedia.org/wiki/C._E._Hooper.

209 **In a complete revamping of their marketing strategy:** Ilan Brat, "The Emotional Quotient of Soup Shopping," WSJ.com, February 17, 2010. http://online.wsj.com/article/NA_WSJ_PUB:SB10001424052748704804204575069562743700340.html.

211 **"Most Brands Still Irrelevant on Twitter":** http://adage.com/digital/article?article_id=145107.

222 **Date: Wed, 22 Jul 2009:** Tony Hsieh, "CEO Letter," Zappos.com, July 22, 2009. http://blogs.zappos.com/ceoletter.

224 **The 2010 Grammys experienced a 35 percent hike:** http://www.variety.com/article/VR1118014540.html?categoryid=14&cs=1&nid=4749.

SELECTIONS FROM THE COVER DESIGN CONTEST

I want to express a very special thank you to everyone who submitted a jacket design for the book. When I announced that I would be holding a jacket-design contest, I suspected that I was setting myself up to make some tough decisions. You didn't disappoint—the range of creative ideas from which I had to choose was mind blowing. In the end, I felt that Owen Song's simple yet powerful design best reflected the spirit of the book, and I am honored to have the chance to showcase his work.

I am massively grateful to everyone who took the time to share his or her ideas and talent.

Eric Doggett, Austin, TX
@ericdoggett (© 2010 Eric Doggett Studios)

THE COOL TAGLINE WILL GO UP HERE!

the
THANK YOU

ECONOMY

GARYVAYNERCHUK

Best Selling Author of CRUSH IT!

Jamie Dennis, Bradenton, FL @sarno (© 2010 Jamie Dennis)

Veneranda Giarrusso, Montreal, QC
Canada
@venerandag
(© 2010 Veneranda Giarrusso)

Sara Allen, New York, NY @saraballen
(© 2010 Sara Allen)

Los Angeles, CA
@Twitter handle kepano
(© 2010 Stephan A.)

Nate Burgos, Chicago, IL
@designfeast (© 2010 Nate Burgos)

The attitude of gratitude is good for life, business and

The Thank <u>You</u> Economy

gary vay • ner • chuk

By the best selling author of *"Crush It!"*

Thank You **Economy**

*TOP NOTCH MANNERS
FOR TOP NOTCH CONSUMERS*

gary vay • ner • chuk

Menachem Krinsky, Los
Angeles, CA @MKrinsky (© 2010
MenachemKrinsky.com)

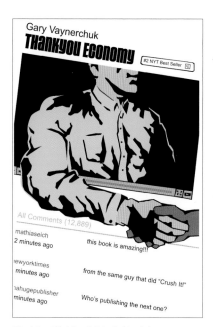

Mathias Eichler & Mark Marlsbary
Olympia, WA @einmaleins
@dsprinting (© 2010 Mark Malsbary)

Mark Macdonald, Toronto, ON, Canada
@mark_macdonald
(© 2010 Mark Macdonald)

Konstantin Ficklscherer, Montreal, QC
Canada (© 2010 Konstantin Ficklscherer)

Jay O'Brien, Kansas City, MO
@JayTheDesignGuy (© 2010 Jay O'Brien
and "JayTheDesignGuy.com")

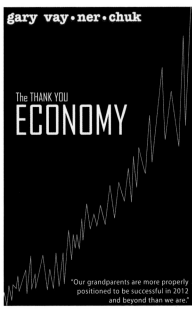

Emmanuel Douskos, Montreal, QC
Canada @mannyd8
(© 2010 Emmanuel Douskos)

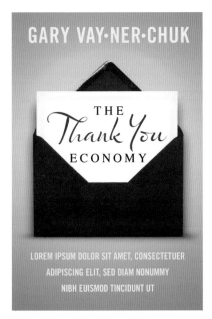

Dustin Bocks, Los Angeles, CA
@mrbocks (© 2010 Dustin Bocks)

Duane B. Thomas, Hurricane, WV
@edyoucation (© 2010 Duane B. Thomas)

Andre Ivanchuk, Syracuse, NY
@AndreIvanchuk (© 2010 Andre Ivanchuk)

Anders Nilsson
Karlstad, Sweden
(© 2010 Anders Nilsson)

Adriano Marinelli
Niagara Falls, ON
Canada
@marinellisauce
(© 2010 Adriano Marinelli)

Vasco Conde
Lisbon, Portugal
@vconde
(© 2010 Vasco Conde)

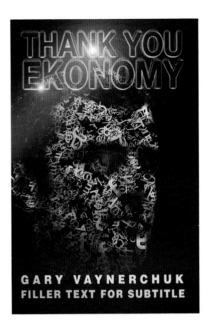

THANK YOU EKONOMY

GARY VAYNERCHUK
FILLER TEXT FOR SUBTITLE

Valentino Ristevski, New York, NY
@valentinoad (© 2010 Valentino Ristevski)

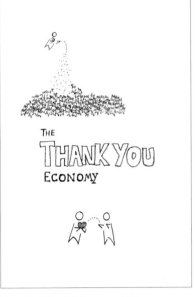

THE THANK YOU ECONOMY

Yew-Wei Tan, Melbourne, VIC
Australia @TanYewWei
(© 2010 Tan Yew-wei's scrivle.com)

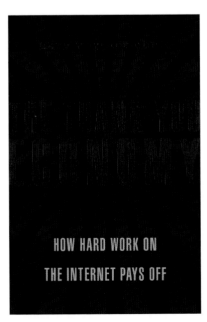

HOW HARD WORK ON
THE INTERNET PAYS OFF

Thomas Reggi, New York, NY
@thomasreggi (© 2010 Thomas Reggi)

Shannon Kienbaum, Chippewa Falls, WI
@shannymk (© 2010 Shannon Kienbaum)

Allen Kessler, Belize @livinginbelize
(© 2010 Retirement Property in Belize)

Ryan Martin, Sugar Land, TX @ruyguy
(© 2010 Ryan Martin)

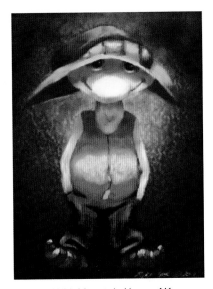

Robert Wahl, Mountain Home, AK
(© 2010 Robert Wahl)

Rachel Walker, Barboursville, WV
@nucgirl1
(© 2010 Rachel Walker)

Richard H. Biever, Evansville, IN
@copperlioninc
(© 2010 Richard H. Biever)

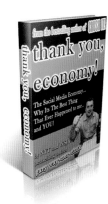

Issamar Ginzberg
New York, NY
@RabbiIssamar
(© 2010 Rabbi Issamar
Ginzberg)

Paula Magnuson
Calgary, AB, Canada
@8thVibe
(© 2010 Paula Magnuson)

Melissa Barrett
Babylon, NY
Facebook: Mbarrettdesign
(© 2010 Melissa R. Barrett)

Lynne Conrad, Mactaquac, NB, Canada
@activ8business (© 2010 Lynne Conrad)

Lorenzo Araneo, New Jersey
@screaminlunatic (© 2010 Lorenzo Araneo)

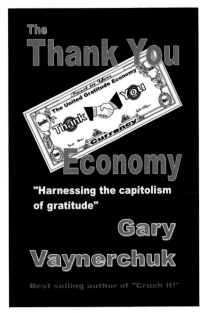

Kashif Pasta, Surrey, BC, Canada
@kashifpasta (© 2010 Kashif Pasta)

John Lawson, Atlanta, GA, @ColderICE
(© 2010 John "ColderICE" Lawson)

Jesse Desjardins, Paris, France
@jessedee (© 2010 Jesse Desjardins)

Jeremiah Nycz, @fireproofdesign
(© 2010 FireProof Designs, Jeremiah Nycz)

From the author of the best seller,
Crush it!
gary vay·ner·chuk

the

thank
you!

economy

Lisofi rdkfiaal fdjkl fjea lkao j;aejflaf!

Jamie Freitas, Norwalk, CT @jsfgraphic
(© 2010 Jamie Freitas)

Gerald J. Daniele, East Hanover, NJ
@TheGreatWazu (© 2010 Gerald J. Daniele)

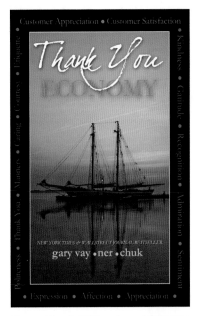

George Marsh, Williamsburg, VA (© 2010
George Marsh WolfpawPhotography.com)

David Behm, Chicago, IL @hint_of_lime
(© 2010 David Behm)

Eric Leebow, NYC/Cleveland/Miami
@EricLeebow (© 2010 Eric Leebow)

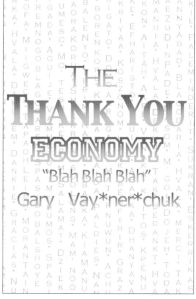

Darrin Brege, Brighton, MI @MickMorris
(© 2010 Darrin Brege)

C.J. Hallock, Kingsport, TN @Cjhallock
(© 2010 C.J. Hallock)

Chris Overcash, Philadelphia, PA
@covercash (© 2010 Chris Overcash)

Capt. Rob Lee @CaptRobLee
(© 2010 Captain Rob Lee)

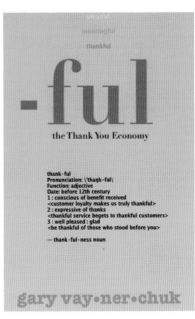

Brian C. Singer, Washington, DC
@theapptree (© 2010 Brian Singer)

Ben Requena, Raleigh, NC
@benrequena (© 2010 Ben Requena)

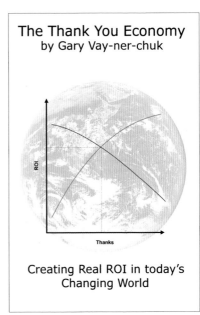

Brian Wing, Rohnert Park, CA
@norcalwingman (© 2010 Brian Wing)